Home
Landscaping

Countryside
Books

A. B. Morse Company
200 James Street
Barrington, Illinois 60010

Where to find

Copyright © 1974 by Countryside Books
A. B. Morse Company
200 James Street
Barrington, Illinois 60010

ISBN: 0-06-4650359

pages 4—13

what is home landscaping?

What can landscaping
do for your home?
Plant materials—
what they are as
described in this
book.

pages 14—29

planning

Plan first,
then plant.
Steps the
amateur
landscaper
can take
to help him
avoid frustrating—
and perhaps
costly—
planting
mistakes.

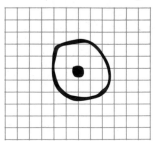

it

plant materials

There are hundreds of different kinds of trees,
shrubs, ground covers, vines, and hedges
from which you may choose *permanent* plantings.
This section shows more than 300 examples
and simplifies selection.

trees

shrubs

ground covers, vines, hedges

details

All of the
information
you seldom find
grouped together
climate zones,
dimensions to
help you plan,
plant materials
by functions,
public gardens
and arboretums,
books, planting,
pruning, feeding,
things that
can go wrong,
glossary,
and index.

what is home landscaping?

Landscaping, or landscape architecture, is the work of planning, designing, and supervising the planting of a land area usually containing a building. A landscape architect decides how to create a landscape that will be pleasant to look at and to live in. He decides what should be planted and where it should be planted. Glorified gardening? Perhaps, but most people consider gardening as the work of only maintaining a landscape or a flower or vegetable garden that's already there.

For the readers of this book, the landscape will most likely be made up of a house, the property it is built on, and the *permanent* plant materials that will be placed on the property. Also included in the landscape will be a location for flower and vegetable gardens.

What are permanent plant materials? They are all of the things that, once planted, are meant to stay where they are. Important among them are trees, shrubs, some ground covers, vines, and hedges. While some permanent plants drop their leaves in the fall, they all retain their woody structure year-round. They don't die down to the ground.

Spring leaves are not yet large enough to hide the permanent structure of the tree at far left. Bare branches of the Boston ivy (above) will form winter patterns against the brick wall.

why landscape?

The purpose of home landscaping is twofold.
1 To set off your house to its best advantage.
2 To create a useful area of beauty around the house for enjoyment by its occupants and neighbors.

The plant materials around your house can affect its appearance. They can make your house look higher or lower than it really is, they can soften unattractive angles, and they can hide an ugly foundation.

Does your house look like a box that's been dropped on the lot? If it does, you can arrange plants around it to make it look as though it belongs on the lot. If you get carried away with too much planting, however, you can make the house look as if it's in the middle of a brush pile.

The owner of a brand-new house knows that there's nothing attractive about a house in the middle of an expanse of raw ground. Even a well-cared-for lawn is more attractive with trees, shrubs, and flowers added. If you are lucky enough to own a wooded lot and your builder has not destroyed the trees unless absolutely necessary, good for you! If you haven't been that fortunate, you will have to take steps to remedy the situation.

This book isn't intended to make you a professional landscape architect. If you want to verge on professionalism, read some of the books listed on page 139. Then consult your local library.

If you live near one of the large public gardens or arboretums listed on page 139, you can use it as a valuable, living reference place. There you can find out how plants will look when they're fully grown, whether certain plants will grow in your area, and how to care for them. You may also discover that classes in landscaping are available in your area. Your local nurseryman or garden center may know of landscaping and gardening classes.

plant size

A public garden or arboretum will give you a means of checking the mature size of trees and shrubs. You don't want to locate the center of an evergreen three feet from the wall of the house if that evergreen will grow to be eight or nine feet wide. It won't look good with one side trimmed off! A shrub that reaches a mature width of five feet won't do if it's planted one foot away from your entrance walk. Your guests won't enjoy doing the hurdles to get to your front door.

The plant materials section of this book, pages 30 through 123, gives mature heights of plants but not widths. Width can vary greatly, depending on the environment in which the plant grows. That's why this book doesn't show widths. You should look at examples of mature plants *in the area in which you live* so that you can see for yourself what size your plant will be when fully grown. Again, check an arboretum or public garden and your local nurseryman or garden center.

plant materials

You can't create a successful landscape without the right conditions — soil, plants, water, food, sunshine, and favorable climate. The *plant materials* you choose are most important to the final appearance of your landscape.

There are, literally, thousands of plants to choose from. But all of them can be organized into a few major categories. This book concerns itself with three categories.

1 Trees
2 Shrubs
3 Ground covers, vines, and hedges

These three categories are *permanent plantings.* They are woody plants.* That is, unless the plant dies or is purposely removed, it will probably stay in the spot where you planted it, year after year. Its woody structure remains all year. Most of this book is about permanent plants. You'll find some nonpermanent plants — the herbaceous* plants, such as the hosta in the picture at right — in this book. But there are other *Countryside Books* that deal with these plants — the annuals,* biennials, * perennials,* vegetables, and house plants.

In the plant materials section of this book, pages 30 through 123, plants are grouped according to their function in the home landscape. Trees are used for shade or for ornamentation because of their shapes or their appealing flowers. Shrubs are chosen for their flowers or their shapes and for their size. Ground covers, vines, and hedges are used to unite other elements of the landscape and in problem areas.

The best basis for selection of plant materials is function and appearance. This book groups plants of similar habits together in the plant materials section to help simplify your selection on that basis. In that section, both common and scientific names are given for each plant. In the index, pages 141-144, you'll find an alphabetical list of the common names of all plants illustrated in this book and also an alphabetical list of scientific names.

*An asterisk following a word in this book means that the word or term is defined in the glossary, page 142.

Here are three important terms that relate to plant materials. There are others in the glossary on page 140.

Deciduous — A deciduous plant loses its leaves, flowers, and fruit at a certain time of the year. Oaks, maples, and fruit trees are all deciduous plants, as are many other trees and shrubs.

Evergreen — Evergreen plants retain their leaves the year around. Most people are aware of only the needle-leaf evergreens, such as spruce, hemlock, Scotch pine, and yews. There are also broad-leaved evergreens, such as boxwood and rhododendrons.

Hardiness — The hardiness of a plant is its ability to live through extremes of heat and cold. Remember that *every*thing won't grow *every*where. We say that a certain plant is "hardy to temperatures of 20 degrees below zero." This means that the plant is not likely to survive the winters if it's planted where temperatures fall below -20° in the winter. Plants may also be limited in their ability to survive very hot temperatures.

The plant hardiness map on pages 124-125 shows the United States and Canada divided into numbered zones. Each listing in the plant materials section includes the numbers of the zones in which each plant is likely to survive

normal temperature extremes. Find on the map the hardiness zone that you live in, then check the zone limits for the plants that you want to use.

You'll be the one to decide what plant materials will best serve you on your property. You may want to concentrate on plants native to the countryside where you live. Consult your local nurseryman or garden center if you aren't sure what these plants are. Of course, you may also choose plant materials that are native to other areas.

scientific names

Why are Latin (scientific) names used by plant-lovers? Do they use them simply to show off their learning? Perhaps, but Latin names have a real purpose. The same plant may have different common names in different places. But the scientific name stays the same, no matter where you are, no matter what language you speak. When the scientific name of a specific plant is used, there will be no doubt about which plant is being discussed.

For example, the silver maple may be known in various parts of the country as the soft maple, white maple, river maple, water maple, or swamp maple. But use the scientific name *Acer saccharinum,* and there'll be no doubt what maple tree you're talking about. If you've just planted a Schneck oak and your neighbor has put in a Texas oak, would you realize that you've both planted *Quercus shumardii?*

Carl von Linné, a Swedish botanist known as Carolus Linnaeus because he wrote in Latin, developed the first systematic method for naming all plants and animals. His system is still the basis of our modern-day classifications. Why did he use Latin? Because it was the universal language of scholars in his day. It may be a dead language, but it is still used to name living things.

Linnaeus developed two-part names for all known plants. The first name states the genus or group of plants to which a particular plant belongs, the second name shows the species or particular type of plant within the genus. Modern-day usage often adds a third name, which shows a variety within a species. It works as shown below.

Common and scientific names

Maple tree   *Acer*
genus to which all maples belong

Norway maple   *Acer platanoides*
genus, species

Columnar Norway maple   *Acer platanoides* 'Columnare'
genus, species   variety

Typical listing in plant material section

common name————————Columnar Norway maple

scientific name———————— *Acer platanoides* 'Columnare'

description———————— This narrow form of the Norway maple is excellent for street planting, narrow strips, or as an accent.

height at maturity———————— *height to 50 feet*

hardiness zones———————— *zones 4 to 8*

trees

Trees provide shade, floral beauty, brilliant color in autumn, windbreaks, and a means of modifying house appearance. Consider all of these things when selecting trees for your homesite. As you browse through the trees section, pages 30-53, you'll find trees grouped in the following way.

deciduous/evergreen/flowering

When you select your trees with specific purposes in mind, you will probably derive the greatest satisfaction from your plantings. Pages 134-135 list trees according to various specific purposes. On pages 30-31, you'll find details about trees — their shapes, bark, leaves — you may want to consider when you choose.

shrubs

What's the difference between a shrub and a tree? Generally, a shrub is shorter than a tree and its foliage is denser than a tree's and grows closer to the ground. A shrub has several stems instead of one trunk. Some plants can double as small trees or large shrubs — depending on how they're treated. Shrubs can be used as "one of a kind" plantings, planted in groups as privacy screens, and in many other ways. On pages 54-97 shrubs are grouped according to function and appearance in the following way.

flowering/nonflowering

Check the lists of shrubs for various specific purposes on pages 135-137 and information on pages 54-55 about shapes and other details to help you choose shrubs.

ground covers, vines, hedges

Are there spots in your lawn that have "eaten" bushels of grass seed and fertilizer and weed-killers without visible improvement? Try ground cover. Got a stone wall that makes you feel like a prisoner? How about covering that wall with a vine? Do you object to having your wife leered at by the playboy next door when she sunbathes in the backyard in her briefest bikini? A good, thick hedge should make you feel better. The plant materials in this section can help you solve these and other problems.

The lists on pages 137-138 will help you select ground covers, vines, and hedges for specific purposes and growing locations. The material on pages 98 and 99 will fill you in on some details about these landscape problem-solvers that will make your choice more simple.

details

The root system you don't see is a most important part of every plant. In addition, there are many important parts you *do* see. These parts will influence you the most as you choose plant materials for your home landscape.

The structure of a plant — its trunk, limbs, twigs — determines its shape and size. On this structure, the plant's leaves grow. The detailed nature of a plant's leaves and how they are arranged on its structure determine the appearance of the plant.

The leaves illustrated on this page are xerographic copies of actual leaves, actual size. Think of the different types of shade and texture that would be provided by a tree covered with large, broad leaves like the maple leaf and by a tree with small, narrow leaves like the locust. Think of the fall colors of leaves.

Evergreens hold their leaves all winter long. No fall colors there — no details of structure. But details of evergreen leaf shapes vary as widely as do those of deciduous leaves. How different are the appearances of the yew and the juniper leaves at the right! The variety of textures available in evergreen plantings is nearly endless.

maple

juniper

yew

locust

it's easier to revise a plan than a planting

Don't accept your first plan. Consider it. Are you thoroughly satisfied with it? If you aren't, change it. Revise your plan over and over — it's easier than revising a planting.

Sure, you can move plants after they've grown. The globe arborvitae at the left can be dug up and moved, but it's hard work. Even the mature flowering cherry trees above can be moved, but only by professionals. Remember, though, that it's easier to change a plan on paper than a planting in the ground.

planning

1 What you have

Plan to accept — and accommodate — existing features of your site.

2 Making plans

Plan, revise, plan again, to use every space to best advantage.

3 Plants expand

Plan for growth — like children, plants outgrow their beds.

4 Relate house/ground

Plan to unite your house with the ground — make it belong.

5 Relate plants/plants

Plan your plants so that they'll live together comfortably.

6 Live outdoors

Plan your outdoors as a living room — for relaxation, work, play.

7 Organize space

Plan your space for efficiency as well as for enjoyment.

M ake a plan before you plant.

You know nothing about landscaping and have absolutely no idea where to start? This section is planned to help you.

Plan before you plant. Plan thoroughly and for the long run — for the mature appearance of your landscape. At the left are seven items for you to consider as you plan your planting. Each of these items is developed separately in the 14 pages that follow.

So start reading, then start planning for a landscape that you can enjoy and that will please the eyes of everyone who sees it — not only now but for years to come.

native plants

Plants native to your area need less care. Tough, hardy, native American grasses may be the answer to lawn problems in terms of both cost and care.

soil, surfaces

Will soil support plant life on its own?
Or will it need humus* or compost*?
Is the ground level or sloped? Is drainage good?
Are there bare areas that will need planning for erosion control?

environment

Are pollution sources nearby? You may need to lean heavily on plant materials that are pollution-resistant.

Are you the proud owner of a brand-new house with bare ground around it? Perhaps you've acquired an older house surrounded by plantings that seem to have been chosen to block out not only neighbors but also all light and air.

If your property looks like the picture at left, you can enjoy the landscape as it is. But if you aren't so fortunate — and few of us are — you'll need to plan new landscaping.

The first thing to do is to survey your site before you start to plan for planting. Consider the size and shape of your property, slope of the land, the direction in which the house faces, and spots that may be wet or dry.

Maybe you have a professional survey of your property. If not, use a tape measure to find the exact size and shape of your lot and house. Record the measurements. You'll need them when you make your plan. Other things to be considered are shown below. When you feel that you know your site thoroughly, go to the next steps in landscape planning — making the actual plan and choosing plant materials to complement both your house and each other.

what you have
survey your site to make your plan

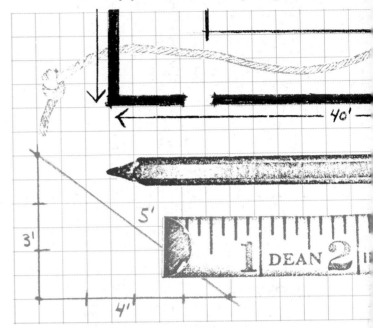

measure

If you don't have a professional survey, use a measuring tape and your memory of geometry to find the exact size and shape of your property. A level mounted in the middle of a long board will help you check surface slopes.

vistas

What you see from your home can be hidden from view or enhanced by planned planting. Decide what you want to see before you plan to plant.

climate

What plant hardiness zone do you live in? What microclimates* do you have?

your dreams

Plan thoroughly. Don't be afraid to drop an unsatisfactory plan and start over. Give some thought to wildlife, too. You'll add color and enjoyment to your life if part of your landscape plan is "for the birds."

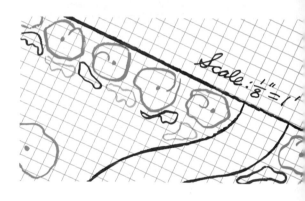

entrances, foundations, corne

Well-planned plantings focus attention on the best features of a house. They soften corner angles and hide unsightly foundations. Plant attention-getting specimens * where they will complement, not detract from, the house.

SCALE: ⅛" = 1'

Scale: ⅛" = 1'

Now that you're well acquainted with your site, start making your plan. You can draw a plan on paper or cut and paste paper shapes to represent plant materials. These shapes may be moved around on a plan of the house and lot for the best effect. You may even want to make a scale model.

Whatever method you choose, you'll need a few basic tools — graph paper, tape measure, ruler, pencils. Examples of different types of plans are shown here.

Consult the measurements of your lot and house, then decide on a scale. Outline the lot on graph paper, then locate the house on the lot. Be sure to indicate entrances and windows. Show walks, drives, service areas, existing plantings, if any. Indicate differences in ground levels. Be accurate — measure carefully, then check your measurements.

Consider the space your plants will need when fully grown — both height and width. Go to public gardens and arboretums to check plant material examples. Or consult your local nurseryman or nearby garden center.

If you're not satisfied with your plan first time around, revise it. Keep on revising it until you *are* satisfied. Changes in the plan are easy. Later, changes of the planting may be difficult or impossible.

making plans

check, consider, revise them

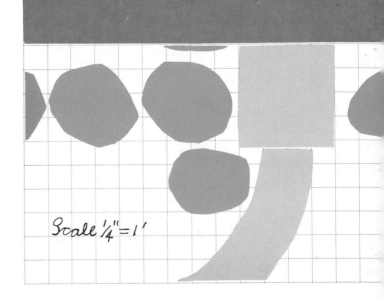

Scale ¼"=1'

pecimens

form, texture, color, detail, height and width

The variety of textures, forms, and colors available to the landscaper is almost endless. Some trees, such as the sweet gum (above, center), can be chosen for both shape and color. The single leaf (below at right) shows the brilliant fall color of the sweet gum.

plants expand
consider both space and time

When locating plant materials on your plan, always keep in mind that trees and shrubs take up space. Plants consume time, too. The more time plants spend growing, the more space they will take. Some grow very slowly, some very fast. The shape of the space taken depends on the plant. Each plant has its own natural form. Consider, too, your own time that will be spent in caring for the plants.

When you select a small plant for your landscape, be aware of and allow for its mature size. The plant materials section of this book shows heights but not widths for each plant illustrated. Width is omitted because it will vary greatly with variation in location. Check your local nurseryman or garden center for probable widths of mature plants.

When planning your landscape, keep variety in mind — variety of form, size, texture, color. A lawn full of nothing but fir trees will look like a Christmas-tree farm.

base plantings

Base plantings should complement your home by drawing attention to its favorable features. Small trees, low spreading shrubs, vines, and ground covers are best (2, 4). Save bright-colored flowers and odd-shaped shrubs for other areas.

What is the focal point of your home? Probably the main entrance. Arrange plants around the base of your house to focus attention on the entrance (1). Plant low growing materials under windows to avoid blocking the view and the light (1, 5).

One more thing — locate trees and shrubs at least half their total mature width away from the house. Then you can wash windows, paint trim, and reach water faucets and electrical outlets without feeling that your plantings have declared war on you.

When plant materials are properly arranged around a house, they make the house belong to its environment (pictures 7, 8). Good planting can accent a house's good features and hide its bad features.

Plants can make your house blend with the landscape and soften the sharp angle where house meets ground (5, 6). They can unite hard-surfaced areas with the lawn (2, 4).

If your house has a monotonous roof line or large areas of blank wall space, a tree or a tall shrub will break the monotony. Plants will soften sharp corner angles of the house (3).

Older houses are often set on high, ugly foundations. Shrubs are ideal to hide these ugly foundations. Think tall, though. Remember — an 18-inch-tall shrub won't hide a 3-foot-high foundation.

relate house/ground

"belonging"—not only for people

8

7

5 6

23

planting for special purposes

Plant shrubs under trees and ground covers under shrubs to unite and complete your landscape.

For privacy plant a hedge of tightly spaced shrubs arranged in a row. Soften a fence or wall with vines or flowers. Remember to plant three or more shrubs of the same kind together — one plant all by itself can get lost in the overall effect.

Plant low shrubs in front of tall ones for a feeling of depth. To avoid row effects in these plantings, mass low shrubs in groups between tall ones.

Plant to frame an attractive view from your lawn. Or create a hidden vista by partial screening — more interesting because only partly visible.

relate plants/plants

plants can be incompatible

Plan for the mature appearance of your landscape. When you choose plant materials to complement your house, consider the plants in relation to each other when fully grown.

As you plan, compare the appearance of the trunk of a single tree growing out of a lawn area with that of the same trunk surrounded by a low ground cover. What about a group of low shrubs planted under the tree? Visualize walking around that clump of shrubs, looking up into that tree.

Make your paper large enough to help you visualize these things. In your plan let the lawn area grow right up to the house in spots. Look through a clump of trees toward a partly hidden view.

As you relate plants to plants, think of them in each season — bare as well as fully clothed.

Always remember that plant materials are the elements for uniting house, ground, and plantings in one eye-pleasing, harmonious whole.

①

②

patio plantings

Trees can supply filtered light and shade (5). Shrubs may add refreshing odors. However, trees that drop messy fruit over the patio will *not* add to your enjoyment of it. If tree branches extend over the patio, remember that while birds are enjoyable creatures to have around, having them directly overhead may not be quite so enjoyable.

Flower beds recessed in the patio or in a border can provide color and fragrance (2, 8), as can flowers in hanging baskets and decorative planters. Keep in mind, though, that flowers and flowering shrubs may attract large numbers of bees — needed by plants but not by people.

Some plants need unpleasant odors to attract pollinating insects. You won't appreciate those odors on the patio. Check your nurseryman on this factor.

③

④

⑤

Plan an area of your property for a private outdoor family room. Arrange trees and shrubs to define this area and to add to your enjoyment of it (pictures 1, 5, 7, 8). Consider the need for paths to and from this area.

If you plan a patio, locate it near the house, with easy access from the kitchen. Make it large enough to accommodate normal-sized groups without crowding.

Service areas are vital. Screen refuse cans, compost piles, wood storage area, and other utilitarian objects with attractive shrubs and flower borders. Locate these areas for efficient access.

Arrange walks and drives to enhance views of house and garden (4, 6, 8). If you have room, a bench at the edge of the garden may be a welcome addition (3).

If you have space for off-street parking, design it to double as a play area. Choose paving materials to help make these useful areas attractive as well.

live outdoors
furnishing your outdoor living room

⑧

⑥ ⑦

①

②

③

④

⑤

contrast, harmony, boldness

Evergreen plantings are enhanced by contrast with deciduous trees or plants (1, 3-5). Enjoy the contrast of exposed and covered portions of brick or stone (7), the contrast of flower plantings with a split-rail fence (8). Don't cover a wall or fence completely with vines or shrubs.

Group plants. Plant three or more shrubs of the same kind together. Don't alternate single specimens — it's not only monotonous, it's confusing.

Let your landscape make bold statements. Long, sweeping curves make a border more interesting than short, choppy curves. A bold splash of color in the midst of a green hedge may be effective (2, 6).

Plan your landscape for year-round harmony and contrast of mass, color, line, scale, and texture. Deciduous trees and shrubs, evergreens, ground cover, flowers, and turf when interestingly related to buildings, walls, walks, and each other are the space-organizing elements that provide landscape interest.

A variety of attractive foliages, forms, and fruit will create interest in periods when nothing is in bloom. In winter leafless branches provide interesting patterns and contrasts with evergreen trees and shrubs (picture 3). You can have color in winter too, such as the red twig dogwood.

Plant flowers or ground cover in front of shrubs and in bays along the border. Several varieties will ensure an interesting border all season long.

Massed bright colors of garden flowers, the fragrance of lilacs, the contrast of texture between a ground cover, such as pachysandra, and the smooth grass of a well-kept lawn — color, odor, texture — use them all to give beauty and interest to your landscape.

organize space

make definite statements

⑥   ⑦

⑧

size, shape, structure, hardiness, details of bark and leaves will all influence choice of trees for your home landscape

details

Sizes, shapes, colors of both leaves and flowers are not the only features of trees to consider. There are many other details. Look at the shagbark hickory trunk at the right in the picture above. Compare this rough, shaggy brown bark with the smooth, chalk-white bark of a paper birch or the smooth, reddish-brown bark of a cherry tree.

Think about the detailed shapes of leaves, too. On page 13 you'll find examples of some typical leaf shapes. If you want to know more about leaf shapes and many other details, check your local library for a copy of the classic *Standard Cyclopedia of Horticulture* by Liberty H. Bailey.

vase   *pyramidal*   *oval*

Trees in this section are organized in three groups, arranged in this order:

deciduous

Trees that drop their leaves in the fall, like the maples at the right, appear on pages 32-43.

evergreen

Trees that keep their leaves all year round, like the needle-leaved Norway spruce at far left, appear on pages 44-45.

flowering

Trees that flower both evergreen and deciduous, appear on pages 46-53.

As you select trees for your home landscape, consider several other things in addition to the fundamental deciduous/evergreen/flowering distinction.

size

Trees expand. When you select young ones, be aware of their size when *fully grown*.

shape

Trees come in a variety of shapes. See the diagrams below. Choose shapes both to create an overall effect and to fit available space.

structure

Most deciduous trees are exposed as "bare bones" in the winter. Branching patterns add winter landscape interest. Evergreens with needle leaves are inclined to modest concealment of their framework the year around.

hardiness

These days you need to consider a plant's ability to survive both natural and man-made environments. If you live in a problem area, select plants known to be pollution-resistant.

trees

round   *spreading*   *columnar*   *weeping*

Shumard oak
Quercus shumardii
An attractive shade tree with an open crown and deeply lobed leaves, shiny dark green above, light green below. The bark is gray or reddish brown. Good for lawn planting.
height to 75 feet
zones 5 to 9

White oak
Quercus alba
A long-lived tree with a stately form. Its leaves are bright green with rounded lobes. Useful as a shade or specimen tree.
height to 100 feet
zones 4 to 9

Japanese maple
Acer palmatum
Graceful and low growing, the Japanese maple works well in borders and in groupings. Foliage is deep red and deeply cut.
height to 20 feet
zones 4 to 8

Pin oak
Quercus palustris

The most popular of all oaks. Easy to transplant, symmetrical, and of rapid growth. Deeply cut foliage turning to crimson and purplish red in the fall. Fine as a specimen.
height to 75 feet
zones 5 to 8

Sugar maple
Acer saccharum

A most beautiful tree for shade and beauty. Of dense, upright growth, its foliage is especially brilliant in autumn, turning to blazing hues of yellow and red.
height to 80 feet
zones 3 to 7

Silver maple
Acer saccharinum

Very fast-growing, soft-wooded tree. Its leaves are deeply cut and silvery white underneath. Its fall color is yellow.
height to 60 feet
zones 4 to 8

Red maple

Acer rubrum

Reddish flowers, red fruit, and brilliant scarlet
and orange fall foliage distinguish this easily
transplanted, rapid-growing maple. Branches develop
low, and form a dense, narrow, crown.
height to 100 *feet*
zones 4 *to* 9

Schwedler maple

Acer platanoides 'Schwedleri'

The young shoots and leaves are a bright purplish
and crimson color. The older leaves change to a
purplish green. Attractive for the contrast of
its foliage.
height to 60 *feet*
zones 4 *to* 8

Norway maple

Acer platanoides

A vigorous, dense, round-headed tree. The leaves turn a pale yellow in the fall. It resembles the sugar maple except its leaves are larger and it does not grow as tall.
height to 60 feet
zones 4 to 8

Variegated-leaved maple

Acer platanoides 'Drummondi'

A Norway maple with a variegated leaf that is green in the center with ivory edging. Symmetrical and round-topped.
height to 30 feet
zones 4 to 8

Crimson King maple

Acer platanoides 'Crimson King'

This beautiful ornamental tree is a form of the Schwedler maple that was selected in Europe for its brilliant crimson leaves. The color is retained throughout the summer.
height to 50 feet
zones 4 to 8

Columnar Norway maple

Acer platanoides 'Columnare'

This narrow form of the Norway maple is excellent for street planting, narrow strips, or as an accent.
height to 50 feet
zones 4 to 8

European mountain ash

Sorbus aucuparia

Very hardy, dense head with fernlike foliage from July till winter. It has clusters of large flowers early — later, bright red berries make it strikingly beautiful.

height to 100 feet
zones 3 to 8

Black gum

Nyssa sylvatica

Fall foliage first turns a dull, dark red and then a brilliant scarlet. Horizontal branches on this large shade tree droop gradually and gracefully. Likes moist sites.

height to 90 feet
zones 5 to 9

Green ash

Fraxinus pennsylvanica subintegerrima

An excellent, fast-growing tree for difficult areas. Withstands drought, excessive moisture, and wind. Fall color is yellow.

height to 50 feet
zones 3 to 8

Marshall seedless ash

Fraxinus pennsylvanica subintegerrima 'Marshall Seedless'

This shapely tree is a seedless variety of the green ash. Resists drought and disease. Especially good in windswept prairie states.

height to 50 feet
zones 4 to 6

ash
elm
ginkgo
gum

Sweet gum
Liquidambar styraciflua

Reasonably fast grower. Odd, corklike bark. Large, green star-shaped leaves that turn to golden and scarlet in fall. A good shade tree.

height to 100 feet
zones 6 to 9

Siberian elm
Ulmus pumila

A hardy variety that is a rapid grower. Adapts itself to unfavorable soils and conditions. Grows well in extremely dry locations.

height to 50 feet
zones 3 to 9

Ginkgo
Ginkgo biloba

The picturesque ginkgo is adaptable to most conditions and is free of insects and disease. Its unique branching and fan-shaped leaves add interest.

height to 60 feet
zones 5 to 9

Lombardy poplar

Populus nigra 'Italica'
Suitable as a background,
along driveways, for screening
outbuildings and unsightly locations.
height to 90 feet
zones 4 to 8

Bolleana poplar

Populus alba 'Pyramidalis'
Leaves are dark green with
silver underside. A much hardier
and longer lived tree than
the Lombardy. Stands erect, tall
and graceful. Beautiful for
screening or backgrounds.
height to 60 feet
zones 4 to 9

Thornless honey locust

Gleditsia triacanthos inermis
Usually grown as a specimen on
lawn or street, the thornless honey
locust provides light shade with
its fernlike foliage. It tolerates a
polluted atmosphere and is often
found near streets or parking lots.
height to 60 feet
zones 4 to 9

Moraine locust

Gleditsia triacanthos 'Moraine'
This thornless, seedless
honey locust grows fast.
The fine foliage allows
plenty of cool shade but
filters sunlight for good
grass growth.
height to 50 feet
zones 4 to 9

Buckeye (Red horse-chestnut)

Aesculus carnea

Dark green foliage and large spokes of light pink to scarlet flowers. Foliage is darker than the white horse-chestnut. Very hardy and desirable for shade.

height to 80 feet
zones 4 to 9

American sycamore

Platanus occidentalis

Favored for its large leaves, erect growth, and patchy white bark as it ages. Plentiful moisture for rapid growth. A beautiful native tree.

height to 100 feet
zones 5 to 9

Corkscrew willow

Salix Matsudana 'Tortuosa'

This willow is characterized by its twisted, branching habit. It likes a damp soil, but will grow well in most soils. Leaves are olive green, narrow, and 2-4 inches in length.

height to 40 feet
zone 3 southward

Weeping willow

Salix babylonica

A large, lacy tree with long branches weeping to the ground. Good for planting near water, in groups of two or three, or for accenting.

height to 40 feet
zones 5 to 9

Wild black cherry

Prunus serotina

Adapted to moist sites. Its spring flowers are white and fragrant. The bitter fruit turns black when ripe. Medium-sized habit with a narrow crown.

height to 60 feet
zones 3 to 9

Copper beech

Fagus sylvatica 'Atropunicea'

This low-branched tree has a change of leaf color throughout the season. It changes from purple to almost black to copper in the fall. The color can be enjoyed well into the month of December. A strong, clean appearance.

height to 75 feet
zones 5 to 8

American linden (Basswood)

Tilia americana

Grows rapidly with a uniform shape. Fragrant creamy white flowers appear after the leaves. Useful as a specimen, particularly in moist sites.

height to 80 feet
zones 3 to 8

Tulip tree

Liriodendron tulipifera

One of our loveliest native trees. Tall growing, straight trunk, with large, irregular leaves that make it ideal for quick shade. Bears numerous yellow tuliplike flowers in spring.

height to 150 feet
zones 5 to 9

Washington hawthorn

Crataegus phaenopyrum

Ornamental tree bearing white flowers during the spring
and orange-red fruit into the fall and early winter.
Foliage changes a crimson-gold during fall months.
height to 30 feet
zones 5 to 9

Redmond linden

Tilia euchlora 'Redmond'

A straight, beautifully shaped
tree between pyramidal and
columnar. Does well in a variety
of soils and climatic conditions.
Crimson-tipped branches add
color in winter.
height to 60 feet
zone 4 southward

Pyramidal linden

Tilia americana 'Fastigiata'

An unusual and desirable tree
because of its pyramidal form.
Abundant foliage creates a dense
shade. Flowers are fragrant.
height to 50 feet
zones 4 to 9

Greenspire littleleaf linden

Tilia cordata 'Greenspire'

A formal pyramidal-shaped tree
of moderate growth. Fragrant
yellow flowers appear in
midsummer. Tolerant of
urban environments.
height to 50 feet
zones 3 to 7

European white birch

Betula pendula 'Roth'

A fast-growing tree with silver white bark that contrasts nicely with evergreens. In fall it has showy foliage colors.

height to 40 feet
zones 3 to 8

Clump birch

Betula papyrifera

This multiple-stemmed paper birch is picturesque with its snowy white bark. The rich, green summer foliage turns clear yellow in autumn. Used for specimen plantings.

height to 40 feet
zones 2 to 8

Amur cork-tree

Phellodendron amurense

Round, short-trunked tree with compound leaves. Older trees have a corky bark. Fall color from yellow foliage and clusters of black berries.

height to 40 feet
zones 2 to 8

trees

birch
cork-tree
golden chain
olive
silk-tree

Russian olive

Elaeagnus angustifolia

A small tree or large shrub with fine blue-gray foliage. Rapid growing, it contrasts nicely with other plants. Effective as a lawn planting.

height to 20 feet
zones 3 to 9

Cutleaf weeping birch

Betula pendula laciniata

This graceful tree has white bark and pendulous branches. The delicate green foliage and deeply cut leaves make it perfect for functioning as a shade and ornamental tree.

height to 50 feet
zones 3 to 8

Silk-tree (Mimosa)

Albizzia julibrissin rosea

A tree of exotic appearance with a low-growing habit and broad crown. In early summer it produces fragrant pink flowers. An interesting tree for specimen plantings.

height to 30 feet
zones 6 to 9

Golden chain

Laburnum vossi

Unusual, low-growing tree with long flower clusters of pure golden yellow. Its wisterialike blossoms appear in May. The leaves are clover-shaped.

height to 25 feet
zones 6 to 8

Black Hills spruce

Picea glauca densata

Usually symmetrical, compact, and bushy.
Foliage varies from green to blue-green.
One of the hardiest of the spruces.

height to 100 feet
zones 3 to 8

Norway spruce

Picea abies

Popular for use as specimens,
windbreaks, screen plants, and
hedges. Fast growing and hardy.

height to 100 feet
zones 3 to 8

Koster's blue spruce

Picea pungens 'Koster'

A form of Colorado blue spruce
with a true blue color. Should be
planted where it has protection
from hot southwest sun and wind.

height to 120 feet
zones 3 to 8

American holly

Ilex opaca

Good in a wide range of soils and climates.
White flowers in early spring. Red berries in winter
on the female plant if it is near a male holly.

height to 60 feet
zones 6 to 9

Eastern hemlock

Tsuga canadensis

Foliage of this evergreen is dark green, lacy, and drooping.
It finds heavy use in shaded areas. Specimen plantings
can be made of both upright and weeping forms. Hedges
of the upright form create privacy where desired because
of the dense growth habit.

height to 70 feet
zones 3 to 8

fir
hemlock
holly
pine
spruce

Douglas fir
Pseudotsuga taxifolia

One of the largest evergreen trees. This attractive tree forms a compact, pyramidal crown. It has dark bluish green foliage and oblong cones.
height to 300 feet
zones 3 to 9

White fir
Abies concolor

The best of the firs and comparable to Colorado blue spruce in showiness. Color ranges from pale blue-green to blue. Has comparatively slow growth, but is very hardy.
height to 150 feet
zones 4 to 8

Eastern white pine
Pinus strobus

A beautiful cone-bearing evergreen. Long, soft bluish green needles with large brown cones. Long lived and vigorous. Useful as a screen or windbreak.
height to 150 feet
zones 3 to 7

Scotch pine
Pinus sylvestris

A fast-growing, irregularly shaped tree. Gray-green, twisted needles. Reddish brown branches and trunk. Good for screen planting or specimen.
height to 75 feet
zones 3 to 8

Austrian pine
Pinus nigra

A vigorous tree that thrives well in cities. Extremely hardy with 4- to 6-inch-long needles. Ideal for windbreak or specimen.
height to 90 feet
zones 4 to 8

Sargent crab
Malus sargentii

Probably the most compact of the crabs. White blossoms are followed by red fruits. Foliage is dark green.
height to 15 *feet*
zones 3 *to* 8

Eleyi crab
Malus 'Jay Darling'

Bronze foliage and bright purple-red fruits make this a favorite among gardeners. Eleyi (left) is a round-crowned tree that produces purple-red blosso in masses, even on young plants.
height to 30 *feet*
zones 3 *to* 8

Prince George crab
Malus 'Prince George'

Has an upright, spreading habit. Blooms late with double rose-pink flowers. Slow growing and produces limited fruit.
height to 15 *feet*
zones 4 *to* 9

Japanese zumi crab
Malus zumi calocarpa

Pink flowers that open to pure white. Bright, round, red fruit. Bushy growth habit.
height to 20 *feet*
zones 4 *to* 9

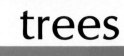

Royalty crab

Malus 'Royalty'

An outstanding variety because of its foliage
and hardiness. Leaves are red, turning purple,
and have a bright, varnished appearance.
Fruits and flowers are dark red.
height to 18 feet
zones 3 to 8

Bechtel's flowering crab

Malus ioensis 'Plena'

Rather slow grower with upright, spreading branches.
Its double pink flowers resemble clusters of small roses.
Round, green fruit.
height to 15 feet
zones 3 to 8

Red Silver crab

Malus 'Red Silver'

Crimson red flowers, small red fruit, and foliage
that is semicut with silver and red color.
height to 15 feet
zones 4 to 9

White Angel crab

Malus 'White Angel'

White blossoms adorn this variety in early spring,
followed by ruby-red berries that last into
the winter months.
height to 20 feet
zones 4 to 9

Chinese redbud

Cercis chinensis

Similar to the native redbud but has denser habit and more flowers.
A spectacular floral display near a patio or among evergreens for contrasting interest.

height to 12 feet
zones 6 to 9

Eastern redbud

Cercis canadensis

The redbud or Judas tree is often used as a specimen or as a high point in a shrub border. Branches are covered with small, purplish pink blossoms before the foliage comes out in the spring.

height to 30 feet
zones 5 to 9

Kwanzan flowering cherry

Prunus serrulata 'Kwanzan'

The upright form of the famous Japanese cherries. An outstanding lawn specimen. Large, double pink blossoms in early spring.

height to 30 feet
zones 6 to 9

Weeping cherry

Prunus subhirtella 'Pendula'

This graceful tree grows rapidly and develops weeping branches that are glorious masses of single or double flowers in the spring. Even when the tree is not in bloom, the cascade effect is delightful and charming.

height to 30 feet
zone 5 southward

Purple leaf plum

Prunus x cistena 'Thundercloud'

The purple leaf plum adds contrast to the landscape scene with its deep purple foliage. Pink blossoms appear in early spring followed by bright red fruits.
height to 10 feet
zones 4 southward

Cherry plum

Prunus cerasifera

A slender tree both ornamental and useful for its sweet, juicy fruit. Flowers are white, fruit red or yellow.
height to 25 feet
zones 4 to 9

Double red flowering peach (Purple Wave)

Prunus persica 'Purple Wave'

One of the most beautiful ornamental trees. In early spring it is completely covered with carnationlike blossoms, followed by green, glossy foliage. A fast grower.
height to 18 feet
zones 6 to 8

Ruby tree

Prunus cerasifera 'Atropurpurea'

This red-leaved flowering plum adds color and contrast. Holds its deep rich color all season. Large pink blossoms in early spring, bright wine-red fruit appears later.
height to 10 feet
zones 4 to 9

Flowering peach

Prunus persica

The lovely double pink flowers of this variety are showy and attractive. Its quick-growing habit and beautiful flowers make it a most desirable lawn tree.
height to 10 feet
zones 6 to 8

Pink dogwood
Cornus florida rubra

Low growing and colorful in the lawn. Before the leaves appear, it is covered with rose-pink flowers touched with bright red.
height to 30 feet
zones 5 to 9

Maytree
(Bird cherry)
Prunus padus

The delightful fragrance of white flowers is only one of this plant's charms. The birds cherish the maytree for the many cherries that ripen in July. In fall it becomes crimson and yellow.
height to 30 feet
zones 3 to 8

Golden rain tree
Koelreuteria paniculata

Does well in a variety of soils, preferring a sunny location. Midsummer brings 12- to 18-inch clusters of lemon-yellow flowers.
height to 30 feet
zones 5 to 8

White fringe-tree
Chionanthus virginicus

Handsome and tall growing. Fragrant clusters of white flowers in May and June. Large green leaves turning yellow in the fall.
height to 25 feet
zones 6 to 9

dogwood
fringe-tree
golden rain tree
maytree
smoke tree

White dogwood

Cornus florida

Beautiful throughout the year. Large, single, white blossoms early in the spring.
Attractive green foliage all summer and dramatic colors
in the fall. Red berries hang on most of the winter. Use as a
specimen, in groups, or as a background for borders.

height to 30 feet
zones 5 to 9

Cherokee Chief dogwood

Cornus florida rubra 'Cherokee Chief'

A truly red dogwood that holds its color throughout the
blooming season. Growth habit similar to pink and
white dogwoods.

height to 30 feet
zones 5 to 9

Smoke tree

Cotinus coggygria

Misty smoke-colored flowers in July.
The feathery flowering appearance
of this shrublike tree is a novel
addition to home landscapes.
The Notcutt variety has purple
foliage and blossoms.

height to 12 feet
zones 6 to 9

Star magnolia

Magnolia stellata

Blooms early in spring, 3-inch fragrant, white blossoms resembling stars. Spreading habit.

height to 15 feet
zones 6 to 9

Southern magnolia

Magnolia grandiflora

Large, slow-growing shade tree keeps its thick, shiny, green foliage year round. Creamy-white fragrant flowers up to 8 inches in diameter are followed by purplish fruit.

height to 100 feet
zone 7 southward

Sourwood

Oxydendrum arboreum

Because of its extremely slow growth, landscapers are beginning to use this tree as a shrub against brick and stone walls in unusual foundation settings. Hanging clusters of fragrant white flowers in summer and red and scarlet fall foliage make it an attractive specimen plant.

height to 50 feet
zones 6 to 8

Sweet bay magnolia

Magnolia virginiana

A fine, specimen plant with glossy, laurellike foliage. Rich, fragrant, white flowers come in June and are followed by attractive red fruit.
height to 15 feet
zones 5 to 9

Saucer magnolia

Magnolia soulangeana

The popular and most hardy magnolia. One of the first to bloom in the spring. Rose-colored blooms accented with white often measure 8 inches across. The Lennei variety is similar, with blossoms of purple on the outside, white on the inside.
height to 15 feet
zones 5 to 9

Magnolia lennei

Magnolia soulangeana lennei

Pagoda tree (Chinese scholar tree)

Sophora japonica

A lovely spreading tree. Flowers in July-September are yellowish white clusters and very showy. Originally from China and Korea.
height to 60 feet
zone 5 southward

Purple flowering saucer magnolia

Magnolia liliflora 'Nigra'

Large lily-shaped flowers of dark reddish purple. Blooms later and longer than soulangeana.
height to 20 feet
zones 5 to 9

variety of forms, flowers, colors, and textures will feed
your imagination as you choose shrubs for your home landscape

details

When you choose shrubs for their flowers, think, too, about *when* they bloom. You might choose shrubs that all bloom in May or June. Then you'll be without color for the rest of the year.

Also consider color of the branches. Shrubs such as the red tw and yellow twig dogwoods can give color to your home landsca even amidst winter snows.

Many shrubs bear colorful fruit that will add interest to your year-round home landscape.

vase   *pyramidal*   *round or globular*

shrubs

Shrubs are grouped in this section in two general categories.

flowering

Both deciduous and evergreen flowering shrubs can be chosen to add beauty to your landscape. Deciduous flowering shrubs appear on pages 56-67, evergreen on pages 68-71.

nonflowering

Deciduous nonflowering shrubs are grouped on pages 72-79, evergreen on pages 80-97. By nonflowering is meant that flowers of these shrubs do not serve a decorative purpose — almost every plant needs to flower to reproduce itself.

There are other things to consider when you select shrubs for your home landscape. In general, the considerations are the same as those involved in choosing trees: size, shape, structure, and hardiness.

Shrubs assume a great variety of forms — vase, pyramidal, round or globular, spreading, columnar, and prostrate — as are shown below. As with trees, shrub forms should fit the space where they are planted.

Shrubs can be grouped in a landscape according to color — of both leaves and flowers. Individual shrubs can be planted to stand alone as specimen plantings.

Again, as with all plant materials, consideration must be given to the environment in which your shrubs must survive. Can the shrubs you choose survive the quality of the air and water with which they — as well as you — must live?

spreading   *columnar*   *prostrate*

Rose of Sharon

Hibiscus syriacus

When few other shrubs are blooming in August and September, these are covered with single or double blossoms. Flowers are purple, red, or white. Fine for specimens, hedges, or background plantings.

height to 10 feet
zone 5 southward

Pink weigela

Weigela florida rosea

An easy-to-care-for plant that bears deep pink flowers in June. Attractive to bees and hummingbirds.

height to 10 feet
zones 5 to 9

Vanicek weigela

Weigela florida vanicek

Flowers of sparkling ruby-red, shading to garnet-crimson. Easy to grow and makes a big June display.

height to 10 feet
zones 5 to 9

almond
beauty bush
crape myrtle
rose of sharon
weigela

Beauty bush
Kolkwitzia amabilis

A handsome ornamental shrub with blush-pink flowers that resemble those of the weigela. Flowers profusely on spraylike branches. Grows well in dry, sandy, poor soils.
height to 6 feet
zones 5 to 9

Crape myrtle
Lagerstroemia indica

Strong growing and hardy except where temperatures often drop below zero. Blooms are large clusters of crinkled florets appearing in late July and August.
height to 20 feet
zones 7 to 9

Variegated leaf weigela
Weigela florida variegata

Lovely light pink flowers but noted for the contrast of the yellow and green leaves. A fine specimen.
height to 10 feet
zones 5 to 9

Flowering almond
Prunus glandulosa

Clusters of double blossoms in May make this a very showy shrub. Varieties have either pink or white flowers.
height to 5 feet
zones 5 to 9

Lynwood Gold forsythia

Forsythia intermedia 'Lynwood Gold'

Originated in Ireland, it has become a favorite. Branches are erect and smothered with golden yellow flowers from top to bottom. Superb for cutting and flowering in the house during winter months. Effective as a mass planting.

height to 8 feet
zones 5 to 8

Golden Bell forsythia

Forsythia intermedia 'Golden Bell'

One of the most popular. Large and bushy with graceful, sweeping foliage. In spring, before leaves appear, the plant is covered with bell-shaped golden blooms.

height to 8 feet
zones 5 to 8

Pink slender deutzia

Deutzia gracilis rosea

Prettiest and most graceful of deutzias. In late May an abundance of pink flowers. Does well in sun or light shade. Excellent for edging walks or foreground of foundation plantings.

height to 3 feet
zones 6 to 8

Lemoine deutzia

Deutzia lemoinei

Slender, upright branches are covered in May with white flowers. Prefers sunny locations.

height to 5 feet
zones 4 to 8

deutzia
forsythia
quince
sweet pepperbush

Flowering quince
Chaenomeles lagenaria

An early bloomer. Upright, spreading with attractive foliage. Blossoms usually from light pink to scarlet. Grows in almost any location and used as a hedge, screen, or specimen.
height to 6 feet
zones 5 to 9

Slender deutzia
Deutzia gracilis

Dwarf habit, dense and bushy. The drooping branches are wreathed with numerous cluster of pure white flowers Ideal as a low hedge in sun or partial shade.
height to 3 feet
zones 5 to 8

Sweet pepperbush
Clethra alnifolia

A neat, compact shrub that blooms freely for several weeks in the summer. Very fragrant white flowers. Prefers moist, acid site.
height to 6 feet
zones 4 to 8

Kalm St. John's wort

Hypericum kalmianum

Low-growing evergreen with narrow oblong leaves. Summer flowering with golden flowers. Useful as a border, ground cover, or foreground.
height to 3 feet
zones 5 to 8

Pussy willow

Salix discolor

A hardy shrub popular for its silvery catkins. Easily forced indoors in late winter and early spring.
height to 15 feet
zones 3 to 9

St. John's wort

Hypericum prolificum

A brilliant mound of gold all summer. Low growing with glossy green foliage.
height to 4 feet
zones 5 to 8

Snow hill hydrangea

Hydrangea arborescens grandiflora

Popularly known as "Hills of Snow." Very showy and low growing. Compact, large attractive foliage. Covered with white snowball-like flowers from early July until late summer. Does well in shade and moist soils.
height to 5 feet
zones 5 to 9

Japanese hydrangea

Hydrangea macrophylla

Vigorous, hardy, roundish plant that does well in shade and acid soil. Flowers are rich blue, pink in alkaline soil.
height to 6 feet
zones 6 to 9

hydrangea
pearl bush
pussy willow
rose acacia
St. John's wort

Rose acacia
Robinia hispida

Pink, sweet-pealike blossoms. Blooms in May and June.
Handsome foliage with red bristly branches.
height to 4 feet
zones 5 to 9

Pearl bush
Exochorda racemosa

An abundance of white blossoms in April.
Used extensively in mass
plantings. Prune severely at planting
time for best results
height to 10 feet
zones 5 to 9

Pee gee hydrangea
Hydrangea paniculata grandiflora

Mammoth flowers in August when few other
shrubs are in bloom. Pinkish white flowers
that gradually deepen to reddish bronze.
Fine for hedges, borders, specimens.
height to 6 feet
zones 4 to 9

Oak leaf hydrangea
Hydrangea quercifolia

Big leaves that resemble the foliage of the oak.
Flowers are similar to the Pee Gee and are borne in
conical heads. Majestic and showy. Brilliant fall
coloring.
height to 6 feet
zones 6 to 9

Chinese lilac
Syringa chinensis
Large, loose heads of reddish purple flowers that appear in June. One of the finest.
height to 10 feet
zones 5 to 7

French hybrid lilacs
Syringa vulgaris
Among the aristocrats of flowering shrubs because of its brilliance. Vary in size and form and come in many colors. Flowers are fragrant, long-lasting, and excellent for cutting. Hardy and demand little or no culture beyond normal care. Use as specimen, hedge, or background.
height to 20 feet
zones 4 to 8

shrubs

honeysuckle
kerria
lilac

Winter honeysuckle
Lonicera fragrantissima

Fragrant, creamy white blossoms in early spring, red berries in late summer. Rich green foliage to midwinter.
height to 10 feet
zones 5 to 9

Tatarian pink honeysuckle
Lonicera tatarica 'Rosea'

Upright with a profusion of small blossoms in May and June. Ornamental red berries cover the bush from summer and usually into winter. Vigorous and easy to grow.
height to 10 feet
zones 4 to 8

Clavey's dwarf honeysuckle
Lonicera x xylosteoides 'Clavey's dwarf

A hardy dwarf shrub with light yellow flowers in May and red berries in fall.
height to 5 feet
zones 4 to 8

Kerria
Kerria japonica

A slender, bright green branched shrub with single, golden flowers in spring. The double flowering pleniflora variety grows to 6 feet.
height to 4 feet
zones 5 to 9

Lemoine mockorange
Philadelphus lemoinei

An upright spreading shrub. It has
fragrant white flowers in June,
borne in terminal clusters.
height to 6 feet
zones 5 to 9

Virginal mockorange
Philadelphus virginalis

Outstanding with large, semidouble fragrant
white flowers. Usually blooms summer through fall.
height to 8 feet
zones 5 to 9

Anthony Waterer spirea
Spirea bumalda 'Anthony Waterer'

An upright, medium low shrub with flat
flower clusters of rose-red in midsummer.
height to 3 feet
zones 4 to 9

Bridal wreath
Spirea prunifolia

An attractive shrub with fine, white flowers
appearing in May. The plena variety
has double flowers.
height to 6 feet
zones 5 to 9

Golden mockorange

Philadelphus coronarius aureus

Bright yellow foliage and fragrant white flowers in May and June. Often used as a border.

height to 6 feet
zones 4 to 9

Sweet mockorange

Philadelphus coronarius

Most common mockorange. Creamy fragrant white blossoms, in late Spring. Very hardy.

height to 10 feet
zones 4 to 9

VanHoutte spirea

Spirea vanhouttei

The most pendulant and full form of spirea. Prolific spring flowering of pure white flowers. Effective as a specimen or hedge. Needs sunny location for good growth.

height to 8 feet
zones 4 to 9

Billiard spirea

Spirea billiardii

An upright shrub with bright pink flower clusters in July and August.

height to 6 feet
zones 4 to 9

Dwarf viburnum

Viburnum opulus nanum

A dwarf plant, well adapted for edgings and hedges in wet or heavy clay ground where other plants fail. Does well in light shade.
height to 2 feet
zones 5 to 9

Viburnum carlesi

Viburnum carlesi

Fragrant white flowers in dense clusters. Bluish black fruit. Good for forcing in winter.
height to 5 feet
zone 5 southward

Wayfaring bush

Viburnum lantana

Vigorous, with soft, heavy leaves and clusters of white flowers in June. Red berries turn black in fall.
height to 15 feet
zones 5 to 8

Common snowball

Viburnum opulus sterile

Distinguished by round, ball-like clusters of snow-white flowers in spring. Plant in well-drained, open location.
height to 12 feet
zones 4 to 8

Japanese snowball

Viburnum plicatum

A rare and beautiful species. Large, globular, pure white flowers that hang long on the bush. Blooms in May.
height to 8 feet
zones 5 to 9

Double file viburnum
Viburnum tomentosum

Used as a specimen or border. White flowers in June
followed by red berries, later turning black.
One of the most beautiful of flowering shrubs.
height to 10 feet
zones 5 to 8

Wright viburnum
Viburnum wrighti

Originated in Japan. Rather large, white
flowers in May and June followed by
large clusters of brilliant red fruits.
These last until fall when foliage turns rich crimson.
height to 8 feet
zones 5 to 9

Arrow-wood
Viburnum dentatum

Glossy green foliage with white flowers
in June; crimson berries turning blue in
autumn. An outstanding shrub for
landscape planting.
height to 15 feet
zones 4 to 8

Highbush cranberry
Viburnum opulus

White flowers in May with brilliant red berries in fall
that remain well into winter. Dark green foliage
turning red in late summer. Hardy and does well in
dry soil.
height to 12 feet
zones 4 to 8

Garland flower

Daphne cneorum

Low-growing evergreen shrub with abundant
rose-pink fragrant flowers in the spring.
Its dense, procumbent habit makes
it useful as a ground cover.

height to 3 feet
zones 5 to 8

Common camellia

Camellia japonica

A tall-growing shrub with large, showy flowers. Long,
lustrous green leaves. Use as a specimen, for screening,
or for espalier techniques.

height to 25 feet
zones 7 to 9

Glossy abelia

Abelia grandiflora

A shrub of medium growth rate. Dense, glossy foliage
covers arching branches that bear petite clusters of
rose-white blossoms from June to October.

height to 4 feet
zones 6 to 9

abelia
azalea
camellia
garland flower
mountain laurel

Mountain laurel

Kalmia latifolia

Dark green evergreen foliage. Clusters of pink to white cup-shaped flowers in May. Adapted to acid soil and shady locations. Excellent for natural landscapes.

height to 10 feet
zones 5 to 9

Kaempfer azalea (Pride of Mobile)

Azalea obtusa kaempferi

Large, orchid-pink flowers literally smother the entire plant. A startling display.

height to 4 feet
zones 7 to 9

Korean azalea

Azalea yedoensis poukhanensis

A compact, low-growing plant with a profusion of fragrant, orchid-lavendar flowers in late May. Evergreen in southern locations.

height to 3 feet
zones 6 to 9

Chinese azalea

Azalea mollis

A deciduous shrub with flowers ranging from orange-yellow to salmon. Excellent flower cover May - June. Grows in sun or shade.

height to 4 feet
zones 5 to 7

Kurume azaleas

Azalea obtusa

Kurume azaleas are hybrids developed in Japan. The profuse blossoms on these compact, dwarf-size plants vary in color from white to pink to deep crimson.
Plant in partial shade. The Snowflake variety has pure white flowers nestled among glossy leaves. The Coral Bells variety, sometimes known as China Rose, produces semidouble flowers of delicate pink.

height to 4 feet
zones 7 to 9

Kurume azalea, Formosa variety

Azalea obtusa amoena

Flowers magenta, often double, in April and May. Hardier than other Kurume azaleas.

height to 4 feet
zones 7 to 9

Kurume azalea hinodegiri

Azalea obtusa hinodegiri

Brilliant scarlet flowers cover this shrub. Dense and compact, this Kurume azalea can also be used as a close, low hedge.

height to 4 feet
zones 7 to 9

Kurume azalea, snow variety

Azalea obtusa snow

The best known of the whites. Especially lovely when used for contrast.

height to 4 feet
zones 7 to 9

azalea
rhododendron

Rhododendrons

Rhododendron

There are over 700 species of rhododendrons of which at least three-fourths are evergreens. For best growth the rhododendrons should be planted in a slightly acid soil and away from the scorching rays of the sun. The following are a few of the more popular varieties of rhododendrons.

height varies, see below; 6 to 35 feet
zones vary, see below; zones 5 to 9

Catawba (Mountain rose-bay)

Lilac-purple flowers in late
spring. A handsome evergreen shrub.
Also in white.
height to 18 feet
zones 5 to 8

Keiskei

A pale, yellow flower in late May to June.
height to 8 feet
zones 6 to 8

Smirnow

White to rose-red flowers in late spring.
height to 18 feet
zones 5 to 9

Carolina

Pale rose-purple flowers in late spring.
height to 6 feet
zones 5 to 9

Rose-bay or Maximum

Rose to purple-pink flowers spotted with green, summer flowering. Large evergreen leaves enhance its appearance.
height to 25 feet
zones 5 to 8

Dwarf barberry (pigmy)

Berberis thunbergi atropurpurea nana

Miniature of the red barberry. Old leaves are bronze blood-red — new growth tips are shades lighter and sparkle in the sun. Fine showing as an edging to walks, in front of shrub planting, or in front of house.

height to 1-1/2 feet
zones 4 to 9

Japanese barberry

Berberis thunbergi

Well-known thorny plant with small yellow flowers in spring, red berries and colorful foliage in fall. Use for foundations, borders, or hedges.

height to 4 feet
zones 4 to 9

Dwarf June-berry

Amelanchier stolonifera

One of the most desirable shrubby amelanchiers. A low-grower with an interesting, irregular branch structure ideal for naturalistic plantings. Creamy white flowers borne in abundance followed by sweet pea-sized purplish fruit.

height to 3 feet
zones 5 to 9

Stephanandra

Stephanandra incisa (Stephanandra flexuosa)

Greenish white flowers in June and July. Foliage turns reddish purple in fall. Winter protection needed in areas north of Kentucky.

height to 8 feet
zones 6 to 9

Red barberry

Berberis thunbergi atropurpurea

Bright red foliage in spring,
brilliant scarlet in fall. Best color, in
full sun. Attractive red berries. Effective
for hedging.
height to 4 feet
zones 4 to 9

Red chokeberry

Aronia arbutifolia

Attractive summer and fall foliage,
showy flowers, and brilliant fruits.
Early May white flowers, followed by
brilliant red fruit in fall. Will grow
in sun or shade.
height to 5 feet
zones 4 to 9

Beauty-berry

Callicarpa dichotoma

Midseason beauty. In August profuse with
closely set pink-tinted flowers. In late September
clusters of violet-purple berries lasting into winter.
height to 4 feet
zones 6 to 9

Floral cotoneaster

Cotoneaster multiflora

An arching bush with clean, blue-green foliage. In late May clusters of hawthornlike white flowers appear along the branches. Large, round, crimson fruits.

height to 10 feet
zones 6 to 9

Rock cotoneaster

Cotoneaster horizontalis

Low growing with forked branches that are almost trailing. Excellent as a gound cover.
Pinkish flowers, followed by red fruit.
Foliage turns brilliant deep crimson in the fall.
height to 5 feet
zones 6 to 9

Alpine currant

Ribes alpinum

A dense, compact shrub that sometimes reaches a height of 8 feet and an equal spread. Can be kept smaller by trimming. Flowers small, followed by bright scarlet berries. Does well in shade and in poor, sandy soils. Excellent hedge plant.

height to 8 feet
zones 3 to 7

Blue mist bluebeard

Caryopteris incana

Perfectly rounded shrub, making a small mound. Covered from August until frost with powdery blue-fringed flowers.
height to 2 feet
zones 7 to 9

bluebeard
cotoneaster
currant
tamarix

Cranberry cotoneaster

Cotoneaster apiculata

Semievergreen, producing single, pink flowers, round, crimson fruit. Use as hedge or as groundcover.
height to 5 feet
zones 6 to 9

Spreading cotoneaster

Cotoneaster divaricata

Pink flowers, branches studded with red fruit in fall and winter. A striking hedge or border.
height to 5 feet
zones 6 to 9

Tamarix

Tamarix africana

Upright with feathery light-green foliage. Small pink flowers are profuse on gracefully bending branches July to September.
height to 10 feet
zones 7 to 9

Gray stemmed dogwood

Cornus racemosa

A free-flowering gray twigged shrub.

height to 8 feet
zones 3 to 8

Yellow twig dogwood

Cornus stolonifera flaviramea

The yellow twig variety has the same habits of growth and characteristics as the red twig variety.

height to 8 feet
zones 3 to 8

Bailey's dogwood

Cornus baileyi

A handsome, erect shrub with dark red branches. Blooms nearly all summer. The fall color of foliage and winter color of twigs are beautiful. Does especially well in sandy soil.

height to 6 feet
zones 3 to 8

Fruitland elaeagnus

Elaeagnus fruitlandi

Fast-growing and hardy. Medium, pointed leaves. Slightly silvery underneath. Silvery bronze berries. Excellent as hedge or screen.

height to 10 feet
zones 7 to 10

Simon elaeagnus

Elaeagnus pungens simoni

Small and compact with rounded, glossy leaves, silvery underneath. Bronze fruit. Low growing, usable for foundations or hedge.

height to 8 feet
zones 7 to 10

Red twig dogwood

Cornus stolonifera

Spreading with red twigs in winter.
Creamy white flowers followed by
white berries.
height to 8 feet
zones 3 to 8

Variegated-leaved dogwood

Cornus elegantissima variegata

Outstanding accent plant. Leaves deep green with
wide border of silvery white. Flowers in early June
with white fruits in late summer.
height to 8 feet
zones 3 to 8

Yeddo euonymus

Euonymus yedoensis

A showy Asiatic shrub with small
yellow flowers in early spring, scarlet
fruit with pink husks in the fall.
height to 8 feet
zones 3 to 10

Winged burning bush

Euonymus alatus

Dwarf and compact with large,
thin-textured leaves that turn deep, warm
crimson in autumn. Corky bark. Thrives in
any soil under most difficult situations.
height to 8 feet
zones 3 to 10

European euonymus (Spindle tree)

Euonymus europaeus

A shrub or small tree. Flowers
yellowish green, more showy than
in other euonymus. Fruit is
four-lobed, red or pink with
orange pods.
height to 20 feet
zones 3 to 10

Potentilla (Cinquefoil)

Potentilla fruticosa

This compact, tightly branched shrub is popular among American gardeners. Most varieties exhibit small, bright yellow flowers, while a few bear white blossoms. An excellent edging or low hedge, providing summer and fall color.

height to 4 feet
zones 3 to 9

Regel's privet

Ligustrum obtusifolium regelianum

A spreading, semiupright shrub with numerous blue-black berries. As a hedge, it makes a fine, graceful planting.

height to 6 feet
zones 5 to 9

Golden ninebark

Physocarpus opulifolius aurea

Exhibiting spirealike growth, the golden ninebark works well in informal borders or hedge plantings. Flowers are very small, but numerous. Easily grown in most garden soils.

height to 8 feet
zones 4 to 9

shrubs

elder
indian currant
ninebark
potentilla
privet
snowberry
witch-hazel

Indian currant

Symphoricarpos vulgaris-orbiculatus
An erect, shrub with white blossoms
in June and July. Attractive fall
color with crimson foliage, red berries.
height to 7 feet
zones 5 to 9

Vernal witch-hazel

Hamamelis vernalis

A multistemmed shrub that has yellow
or reddish flowers in early spring.
Useful for borders or screens. Prefers
moist sites.
height to 6 feet
zones 5 to 8

Golden elder

Sambucus nigra 'Aurea-variegata'
Golden yellow leaves provide interesting
contrast. White flowers in flat-topped
clusters. Grows tall but can be pruned
into a neat, compact bush.
height to 8 feet
zones 4 to 8

Snowberry

Symphoricarpos racemosus
A hardy shrub that does well in shade
and poor soil. Light pink flowers,
June-August. In late summer, attractive
berries appear and last until winter.
height to 6 feet
zones 4 to 9

79

This foundation planting effectively combines pines, junipers, and yews.

Plume cypress

Chamaecyparis pisifera plumosa

Showy green feathery foliage throughout the year. If left untrimmed, it will make a large, graceful pyramid; or it can be trimmed into a smaller, shrub form.

height to 15 feet (average)
zones 5 to 9

Gold thread cypress

Chamaecyparis pisifera filifera aurea

One of the best and most distinctive of the cypresses. Unusual foliage that is drooping and graceful, resembling cords of golden yellow. Compact, pyramidal form, fine color in winter and summer.

height to 6 feet (average)
zones 5 to 9

Pyramidal arbor-vitae

Thuja occidentalis pyramidalis

This is a beautiful columnar, golden-green evergreen that is splendid for accent planting, entrances, or as a living fence.
height to 25 feet
zones 4 to 8

Baker's arbor-vitae

Thuja occidentalis 'Bakers'

A striking evergreen that retains its shape without shearing. Compact and pyramidal with dark green foliage.
height to 10 feet
zones 6 to 9

Globe arbor-vitae

Thuja occidentalis globosa

The nearest in form to a perfect globe. A lovely, useful evergreen, with dark green, dense, dwarf growth. A useful accent plant.
height to 3 feet
zones 4 to 8

Bonita arbor-vitae

Thuja occidentalis 'Bonita'

Now widely grown, this variety has a dwarf, round form with dark green foliage. Compact and distinct in habit, ideal for foundation planting.
height to 5 feet
zones 6 to 9

Golden arbor-vitae

Thuja orientalis aurea-nana

A compact variety with yellow spring foliage. Especially useful for brightening foundations.
height to 5 feet (average)
zones 6 to 9

Bird's nest spruce
Picea abies nidiformis
A dwarf that is hardy, robust, and fairly slow growing. Ideal for rock gardens and to give an oriental feeling.
height to 3 feet
zones 4 to 8

Moffett juniper
Juniperus scopulorum 'Moffettii'
Bright bluish foliage and compact upright growth characterize this juniper. Requires little shearing to retain its symmetrical shape.
height to 25 feet
zones 5 to 9

Canaert juniper
Juniperus virginiana 'Canaertii'
Rich, dark green foliage. Small, blue berries add to its beauty. Very hardy. Compact, pyramidal habit.
height to 10 feet (average)
zones 4 to 9

Cologreen juniper
Juniperus scopulorum viridifolia
This is one of the best Colorado or Rocky Mountain junipers. An upright tree with excellent form. Especially beautiful for its bright green foliage.
height to 40 feet
zones 5 to 9

Andorra juniper

Juniperus horizontalis plumosa

Grayish green foliage in summer, changing to a lavender-orchid color in fall and winter. Its low growing habit is ideal for use as a ground cover.

height to 2 feet
zones 3 to 9

Tamarix juniper

Juniperus sabina tamariscifolia

A small, compact spreading juniper with blue-gray foliage. Ideal for mass planting where a low-growing effect is wanted.

height to about 18 inches
zones 5 to 9

Japanese juniper

Juniperus procumbens

Low, prostrate growth, often used as a ground cover. Needle-type blue foliage that curves upward. May require annual trimming to control growth habit.

height to 30 inches
zones 4 to 9

Rocky Mountain juniper

Juniperus scopulorum

Compact and symmetrical, with bright, light bluish foliage. Unlike many evergreens, this becomes brightest during summer months.

height to 10 feet
zones 5 to 9

Dwarf pfitzer

Juniperus chinensis pfitzeriana compacta

Comparatively slow grower with foliage lighter green than the regular pfitzer. Its compact pyramidal habit is ideal for limited space.

height to 30 inches
zones 4 to 9

Silver cedar juniper
Juniperus virginiana 'Glauca'

The compact, conical shape combined
with its silvery foliage makes this
a desirable plant.
height from 10 feet
zones 4 to 9

Spiny creek juniper
Juniperus excelsa stricta

A very compact, cone-shaped plant,
with dense, spiny, blue foliage.
Prefers dry, sunny location.
height to 10 feet
zones 5 to 9

Dundee juniper
Juniperus virginiana 'Dundee'

A compact, pyramidal
evergreen. Bluish green
summer foliage turns
attractive plum color
in winter.
height to 10 feet
zones 4 to 9

Meyer juniper
Juniperus squamata 'Meyeri'

An evergreen of unusual beauty.
Foliage is pointed, prickly, and
of bright, shiny blue.
height to 5 feet
zones 5 to 9

Von Ehren juniper
Juniperus sabina 'Von Ehren'

Vase-shaped spreading evergreen with
feathery dark green foliage.
height to 6 feet
zones 3 to 9

Hetz juniper
Juniperus chinensis 'Hetzii'

This form of juniper has graceful
habit and rapid growth. Has a
pleasing silvery blue color.
height to 5 feet
zones 3 to 9

Maney juniper
Juniperus chinensis 'Maney'

Compact and spreading with bluish foliage. Does well in light shade.
height to 3 feet
zones 4 to 9

Armstrong juniper
Juniperus chinensis 'Armstrongii'

Fine gray-green foliage and very compact. Useful for foundation planting and will tolerate some shade.
height to 4 feet
zones 5 to 9

Attractive foundation plantings can be made combining evergreens and deciduous shrubs.

Burk juniper

Juniperus virginiana 'Burkii'
Dense steel-blue foliage that becomes
reddish in fall. Naturally compact.
May be sheared annually.
height to 10 *feet*
zones 5 *to* 9

Ames juniper

Juniperus chinensis 'Ames'
A broad, pyramidal form
that tapers to a point.
Outstanding blue-green
color. Best in full sun.
height to 10 *feet*
zones 3 *to* 9

Irish juniper

Juniperus communis hibernica
An erect, columnar form with gray-green
needlelike foliage. Especially useful
at corners and entrances. May be sheared
to prevent growth to full height.
height to 10 *feet*
zones 5 *to* 9

Vase juniper

Juniperus communis depressa
A vase-shaped form and a low-spreading habit.
Attractive, grayish green, sharp needles. This
semidwarf evergreen is a rapid grower.
height to 4 *feet*
zones 3 *to* 9

Upright yew
Taxus cuspidata capitata

Good for hedge or semiformal specimen. Disease
resistant and does well on a north exposure.
Deep green needle foliage and scarlet berries.
height to 12 feet
zones 5 to 9

Dwarf yew
Taxus cuspidata nana

Very slow grower. Low, irregular,
and picturesque outline. Useful as
specimen, hedge, or edging.
height to 3 feet
zones 5 to 9

Slow-growing yews of rich, dark green color
are ideal for foundation planting. They withstand
shearing well and thrive in shade.

Brown's yew
Taxus media 'Brownii'

Normally grows taller than spread.
Short, deep, rich needles. Excellent
for hedge or trimmed in globe shape.
height to 5 feet
zones 5 to 9

Hick's yew
Taxus media 'Hicks'

Branches that ascend vertically for a
columnar tree. Dark, rich green, and
resistant to heat and drought. Holds
color all winter.
height to 6 feet
zones 5 to 9

Densiformis yew
Taxus cuspidata densiformis

The compact form of the Japanese yew.
Vigorous and able to withstand severe winters.
height to 3 feet
zone 4 southward

Ward's yew
Taxus media 'Ward'

A low-growing, spreading yew. Good
foliage color. Relatively disease resistant.
height to 3 feet
zones 5 to 9

Boxwood

Buxus sempervirens

The common box has many forms ranging from weeping, pyramidal, or globe-shaped to treelike varieties. Leaves are rounded and lustrous green. The shrub is easily pruned for hedges or topiaries. Finding increased favor with gardeners is Buxus microphylla, a small-leaved plant that rarely grows over 3 feet, and the variety koreana that rarely exceeds 20 inches.

height to 15 *feet*
zones 6 to 9

Little leaf box

Buxus microphylla

Boxwood and azalea

Mugo pine

Pinus mugo mughus

A low-growing mound habit useful in foundation and rock garden plantings.
Slow growing with bright green
needles. Adaptable to a variety of soils.
height to 4 *feet*
zones 3 to 8

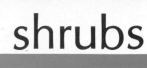

shrubs

boxwood
leucothoe
osmanthus
pine
viburnum

Holly osmanthus

Osmanthus ilicifolius

Use as a specimen or clipped as a tall hedge.
Small, fragrant white flowers in the summer,
followed by bluish black berries. Leaves are
dark green, resembling holly. Use in sun or
partial shade. Likes acid soil.
height to 15 feet
zones 7 to 9

Drooping leucothoe

Leucothoe catesbaei

A medium-growing shrub with lustrous, dark green leaves
turning red or bronze in winter. In late spring it has
3-inch-long pendulous white flowers.
height to 5 feet
zones 5 to 9

Leather leaf viburnum

Viburnum rhytidophyllum

Large, dark green, leatherlike foliage, silver-green
on underside. Clusters of yellow-white
flowers and red berries, changing to black.
Will grow in shade.
height to 10 feet
zones 6 to 9

91

Variegated American holly

Ilex opaca variegata

Ivory-edged leaves make this a unique
form of the American holly. Can be sheared
to desired height. June flowers and
fall red berries.

height to 50 feet
zones 6 to 9

English holly

Ilex aquifolium

Dark green, glossy foliage with pointed teeth along the margins
Bright red clustered fruit. Requires acid soil.

height to 35 feet
zones 6 to 9

Heller's Japanese holly

Ilex crenata 'Helleri'

A dwarf shrub with dense growth and dark,
shiny leaves. Use for foundation planting.

height to 3 feet
zones 6 to 9

Convex leaf holly

Ilex crenata convexa bullata

A spreading plant with dark, shiny green
leaves that are narrow and round in shape.
Black berries. For foundations and hedges.

height to 4 feet
zones 6 to 9

Burford holly

Ilex cornuta 'Burfordi'

A Chinese holly with shiny dark green leaves.
The plant has a mounding growth habit.
Bright red berries that appear in late
summer contrast nicely with foliage.
Likes full sun and moist soil.

height to 7 feet
zones 6 to 8

Big leaf holly

Ilex crenata latifolia

Shiny, dark, elliptical or oblong leaves,
larger than most crenata. A vigorous
plant that grows rapidly and compactly.
height to 20 feet
zones 6 to 9

Round leaf holly

Ilex crenata rotundifolia

Dense foliage with round, glossy green
leaves. Compact habit lends itself to
trimming for foundation or hedge plantings.
height to 3 feet
zones 6 to 8

Japanese pieris (Andromeda)
Pieris japonica

Dark green, shiny leaves. Pendulous clusters of dainty white flowers. Attractive in foundation plantings.
height to 6 feet
zones 6 to 9

East Palatka holly
Ilex opaca 'East palatka'

One of the most abundant bearers of dark red globose fruit. Small glossy leaves. Upright conical form.
height to 40 feet
zones 6 to 9

Variegated wintercreeper
Euonymus fortunei argenteo-marginatus

Leaves have silvery margins and dark green centers. Often holds leaves through winter. Thrives in sun or partial shade. Use as shrub, hedge, or train as vine. Has small, greenish white flowers and pinkish fruit.
height to 15 feet
zones 5 to 9

Emerald 'n Gold euonymus

Euonymus fortunei 'Emerald 'n Gold'

A low shrub of compact growth. Striking green foliage edged
with gold. Useful as a border or foundation planting.
height to 3 feet
zone 5 southward

Erect euonymus

Euonymus fortunei 'Sarcoxie'

An upright columnar bush form that is
excellent for hedges and foundation
plantings. Its dark green, glossy foliage
is held through the winter.
height to 6 feet
zones 5 to 9

Big leaf wintercreeper

Euonymus fortunei vegetus

A graceful evergreen that will grow on walls if planted
nearby. Orange berries in the fall. An excellent hedge
or ground cover.
height to 5 feet
zones 5 to 9

Oregon grape holly
Mahonia aquifolium
Hollylike leaves that change from dark
green to red in the fall. Hardy, preferring
partial shade. Yellow fragrant flowers in
spring followed by blue berries.
height to 4 *feet*
zones 5 *to* 9

Oregon grape holly
Mahonia aquifolium compacta
Attractive appearance through all seasons.
Dark green leaves, red in fall, yellow fragrant flowers
in spring, blue berries in late summer.
Compact habit and uniform shape
make it one of the most desired plants for landscaping.
height to 3 *feet*
zones 5 *to* 9

Leather leaf mahonia
Mahonia bealei
Yellow fragrant flowers in long clusters in early spring. These
are followed by clusters of blue-black fruit. Large leaves
create a dense bushy form. Prefers shade.
height to 12 *feet*
zones 6 *to* 9

Firethorn

Pyracantha coccinea lalandi

A picturesque, upright thorny shrub with
oval evergreen foliage. Has
attractive white flowers followed by a
massive quantity of fiery orange-red
fruits that last well into the winter.
A versatile plant that can be trained
as a hedge or trained in espalier
techniques on walls or fences.
height to 20 feet
zones 7 to 9

there's a ground cover, vine, or hedge to fit nearly every
situation you'll encounter in planning your home landscape

ground covers, vines, hedges

Ground covers unite and complete your landscape. Perhaps more important to you, ground covers provide solutions to many of the head-scratcher problems that home landscapers face. For instance, spots where grass just *won't* grow, no matter what you try. Or along edges of driveways or walks, next to benches or fences, in areas too narrow to mow, in shaded areas under trees. Planted around tree trunks, ground covers will prevent mower damage to trees, hide fallen fruit under fruit trees.

Ground covers are deciduous or evergreen, woody or herbaceous, flowering or nonflowering, and although generally short, they do vary in height. Plan your planting to give a uniform mass of color or plant masses of various ground covers near one another for contrast. But remember that some varieties spread so rapidly that they'll have to be closely watched — otherwise they may walk all over your lawn, into your garden, and under the hedge or fence to visit the neighbor's lawn — which he may not appreciate.

Vines may be useful as ground covers, too. If they are allowed to spread over the ground, they will produce a blanket-like appearance and grow only a few inches tall. But the greatest use of vines comes from the fact that they climb on nearly anything that will stand still long enough for them to grab hold. Vines can relieve the monotony of a bare wall or cover an unattractive dead tree or tool shed. They will provide shade and privacy on a porch or in a screen house.

You can choose deciduous or evergreen vines. They can provide masses of color, with flowers, fruit, or autumn leaves. And many of them require little care — a bonus for you.

Hedges that are wisely chosen and well tended will enhance the value and appearance of your home. Hedges will shelter your outdoor living areas from the wind and from the eyes of strangers. They will provide ornamental borders to frame or create backgrounds for flower beds or to edge walks. They'll provide massed color effects with flowers or foliage. You can clip a hedge to almost any shape for formal effect or let it grow naturally — within bounds — for informality.

Candytuft

Iberis sempervirens

A dwarf perennial plant covered with white flowers in April and May. Very good for edging and rock gardens. Grows well in partial shade.

zones 5 *to* 9

Houseleek (Hen and chickens)

Sempervivum

There are many varieties of this interesting and hardy succulent. Grows well in open sandy places, needs very little moisture. Green, gray, or white thick leaves in rosette clusters; blooms of purple, yellow, or red. Makes an excellent carpet-bedding and grows well in rock gardens, or rock walls.

zones 4 *to* 9

Baltic ivy

Hedera helix baltica

Small-leaved, hardy, evergeen ground cover. Grows well in shady places.

zones 5 *to* 9

Pachysandra

Pachysandra terminalis

A popular ground cover for edging walks, beds, terraces and for banks. Branches freely, forming a dense mat of glossy green foliage. Finds best use under trees and evergreens where shade is dense.

zones 5 *to* 8

ground covers

candytuft
houseleek
ivy
myrtle
pachysandra
pink
thyme

Silveredge (Mother-of-thyme)

Thymus serpyllum argenteus
There are more than 50 species in this
creeping perennial family. Fragrant,
tiny lilac or purplish flower clusters.
Widely grown for its beauty and as
a seasoning.
zones 6 to 9

Cottage pink

Dianthus plumaris
A mat-forming herb with rose-pink,
fragrant flowers, and smooth blue-gray leaves.
Grows best in sunny places.
Spring-blooming flowers that grow
on short stems.
zones 4 to 8

Myrtle (Periwinkle)

Vinca minor
Trailing evergreen that spreads and carpets the ground
under shrubs or trees where it is too shady to grow
grass. Profuse lavender-blue flowers interspersed with shiny green leaves.
Recommended as a ground cover to reduce erosion.
zones 5 to 8

Variegated bishop's weed

Aegopodium podagraria variegatum

A useful foliage plant for edgings and ground cover. This variety has striking white-margined leaflets. Tiny white flowers appear in June, followed by aromatic fruit.

zones 5 to 8

Hall's honeysuckle

Lonicera japonica 'Halliana'

A fragrant, continuous blooming plant for general ground cover. Its excellent root system also holds on steep banks. Thrives in full sun or partial shade. Blooms from spring to frost with large clusters of white flowers. Other excellent varieties are Gold Flame with intense gold-yellow flowers and Red Gold with bright red and yellow flowers.

zones 5 to 9

Red Gold honeysuckle

Lonicera japonica 'Red Gold'

Gold Flame honeysuckle

Lonicera japonica 'Gold Flame'

Plantain-lily

Hosta

A widely grown bushy perennial of the lily family. Grows well in shady or sunny locations and is extremely hardy.

zones 3 to 8

Variegated plantain-lily

Hosta fortunei-marginata-alba

Siebold plantain-lily

Hosta sieboldiana

Dwarf lace plant

Polygonum reynoutria

A low, hardy ground cover with deep red buds opening to pink in late August. Foliage turns bright red in fall. Prolific grower, excellent for banks. Likes sun.

zones 4 to 9

Lily-of-the-valley

Convallaria majalis

Lovely sprays of fragrant white bells bloom in May. Best planted in clumps about 1 foot apart. Will grow almost anywhere under almost any conditions. Especially good in shady places.

zones 4 to 8

Rat-stripper

Pachistima canbyi

A low evergreen shrub preferring sandy, well-drained soil. Trailing habit suited for borders or rock gardens.

zones 5 to 8

Purple leaf euonymus
Euonymus fortunei coloratus

A semievergreen, vining-type ground cover. Lustrous foliage turns purplish red in fall. Especially useful as ground cover for banks or large open areas. An occasional pruning of upright shoots maintains desired mat effect.
zones 5 to 9

Bronze beauty
Ajuga reptans atropurpurea

Planted in full sun, the usually purplish leaves take on a rich bronze color. Will grow equally well in shade or sun. Tiny, deep blue flowers and exceedingly hardy.
zones 5 to 9

Bugle
Ajuga genevensis

Dwarf creeping perennial with dense spikes of blue flowers in May and June. For shady or sunny places. Rich, shiny green leaves. Does not develop runners.
zones 5 to 9

Blue bugleweed
Ajuga reptans

Easy to cultivate and spreads rapidly. Violet-blue flowers on trailing stems. Flowers bloom in May and glossy foliage color all season. Bronze foliage varieties are popular for contrast.
zones 5 to 9

ajuga
euonymus
phlox

Big leaf wintercreeper

Euonymus fortunei vegetus

A truly versatile planting that is a good soil binder and an excellent cover for banks. Graceful evergreen foliage with orange-red berries in fall. A hardy plant and strong grower.

zones 5 to 9

Variegated wintercreeper

Euonymus fortunei argenteo-marginatus

A trailing evergreen vine with silver edge leaves and dark green centers. A very attractive ground cover particularly when planted with solid green vines such as English ivy.

zones 5 to 9

Creeping phlox (Mountain pink)

Phlox subulata

An evergreen creeping perennial that forms a dense mosslike mat. Flowers are prolific in purple, pink, or white. Grows in dry, full-sun locations. Effective in rock gardens and borders.

zones 3 to 9

Blue phlox (Wild Sweet William)

Phlox divaricata canadensis

Large, fragrant, blue flowers that bloom in April and May. Creeping stems easily root, increasing size of plant rapidly.

zones 4 to 9

Viola
Viola cornuta

Large pansylike flowers provide
color from spring to fall. This perennial plant will
form clumps up to 2 feet in diameter.
zones 3 to 8

Oregon grape holly (Mahonia)
Mahonia aquifolium

A low-growing evergreen shrub. Flowers are yellow and
dense in spring, followed by small, bluish berries.
Lovely bronze foliage in fall.
zones 5 to 8

Silver king
Artemisia albula

A unique plant with feathery, frosted
leaves. Its misty look adds beauty and
charm to its location. Grows well in dry,
sandy soil and a sunny location.
zones 4 to 9

Silver mound
Artemisia schmidtiana-nana

A fine, silver-foliaged, mounded plant that
is hardy and prefers sunny, dry areas.
When grouped, it is excellent for edging,
rock gardens, or accent.
zones 3 to 9

cotoneaster
crown vetch
oregon grape holly
sedum
silver king
silver mound
viola

Golden moss
Sedum acre

Sedum (Stonecrop)
Sedum

Most of the 500 species of this low-growing plant are perennial. Valuable for covering dry, sandy areas, this succulent is easy to grow and makes an interesting carpet. Flowers come in red (Dragon's Blood), yellow (acre), white (album), pink (sieboldi), and blue (caeruleum). Dwarf in habit, these thick-leaved plants make interesting edgings and rock garden plants.
zones 4 to 9

Dragon's blood sedum
Sedum 'Dragon's Blood'

Sieboldi sedum
Sedum sieboldi

Cotoneaster
Cotoneaster apiculata

A low-growing shrub with spreading branches. Bright fall crimson berries contrast with shiny green leaves. Dense growth ideal for bank cover.
zones 5 to 9

Crown vetch
Coronilla varia

A spreading, perennial, vinelike plant. Very hardy in sun or partial shade. Pinkish white flowers in dense clusters from early summer until frost. Holds soil on slopes and banks.
zones 4 to 8

Clematis

Clematis

All members of the Clematis genus are either shrubby or woody vines. They are noted for rapid, slender growth, delicate foliage, and a profusion of sweet-scented blossoms through the summer. Clematis do best in rich soil where the roots will be cool and the vines can get sun. They are excellent climbers and decorative for trellises, arbors, and walls. Among the most popular varieties are the jackmani (violet-purple), paniculata (white), montana (white or pink), tangutica (gold), and texensis (scarlet).

zones 4 to 8

Boston ivy

Parthenocissus tricuspidata veitchi

Climbs up to 40 feet and clings firmly to brick or stone walls. Deep green leaves that color to scarlet in fall. Prefers northern or eastern exposures.

zones 5 to 9

vines

clematis
ivy
silver lace
wisteria

Jackmani clematis
Clematis jackmani

Baltic ivy
Hedera helix baltica
A small-leaved variety of the common English ivy. Very hardy, providing a dense cover of dark green foliage.
zones 4 to 8

Wisteria
Wisteria sinensis
A rapid-growing, woody vine that attains a large size. Has long, pendulous clusters of pale blue, lavender, or white flowers in June.
zones 5 to 9

Silver lace vine
(Fleece vine)
Polygonum auberti
A fast-growing, woody vine reaching 20 feet the first year. Greenish white, lacelike, fragrant flowers that bloom heavily from August until late fall.
zones 5 to 9

Big leaf wintercreeper

Euonymus fortunei vegetus

An evergreen vine that grows
well on masonry walls. Bears orange
berries in the fall lasting most of
the winter. Exceptionally hardy.
zones 5 to 9

Variegated wintercreeper

Euonymus fortunei argenteo-marginatus

Leaves have silvery margins and dark
green centers. Often holds leaves through
winter. Thrives in sun or partial shade.
Has small, green-white flowers and
pink fruit.
zones 5 to 9

Bignonia (Trumpet vine)

Bignonia capreolata

A woody, high-climbing
evergreen vine. Flowers summer
to fall, red-orange. Used for
fences, walls, or trees.
zone 6 southward

Bittersweet

Celastrus scandens

A woody vine that is best for low walls
as it is not tall growing. Flowers are
small and yellow, in autumn there are
yellow berries with bright red coats.
zones 4 to 8

Kudzu vine

Pueraria thunbergiana

A fast-growing vine with
small, fragrant purple
flowers. Can climb high and
makes a dense shade with its
broad oval leaves. Excellent
for arbor covering.
zone 7 southward

vines

Akebia
Akebia quinata

A strong, woody, tall-growing vine with small, fragrant, but inconspicuous flowers in spring. Fruit is a purple berry. Useful for shade and on walls or arbors.
zone 6 southward

Bearberry
Arctostaphylos uva-ursi

A handsome evergreen vine with rooting stems. Foliage turns bronze in winter. Fruit is red, flowers white or pink.
zones 3 to 8

Dutchman's-pipe
Aristolochia durior

A woody vine attaining a height of 30 feet and providing shade with large kidney-shaped leaves. Unique brown flowers in the form of a Dutch pipe.
zones 6 to 9

Virginia creeper
Parthenocissus quinquefolia

A vigorous, tall-growing vine with leaves turning to scarlet in the fall. Will form a dense cover and is hardy under most conditions. Thrives best in moist loam.
zones 4 to 9

Buckthorn

Rhamnus cathartica

A large-growing shrub with excellent glossy foliage. Large, shiny black fruits are borne in clusters. A fine plant for a border or hedge, especially popular for its winter color.

height to 25 feet
zones 3 to 9

Tallhedge buckthorn

Rhamnus frangula columnaris

Since its introduction, this plant has found great favor as a tall hedge or screen. Leaves are glossy and stems are thornless. Fruit red changing to black.

height to 15 feet
zones 3 to 9

St. John's wort (Hypericum)

Hypericum hidcote

A good border shrub that will grow to 3 to 4 feet in temperate climates and 18 inches in colder zones. In cool climates it freezes back to the ground but comes up again in spring. The bright yellow cupped flowers are produced in profusion in late spring and last until late fall.

height to 4 feet
zones 6 to 9

Red barberry

Berberis thunbergi atropurpurea

The foliage is bright red in spring, dull red in summer, and brilliant scarlet in fall. For best coloring plant in full sun.

height to 4 feet
zones 3 to 10

hedges

Siberian pea tree
Caragana arborescens

A hardy plant, easily grown,
prefers sunlight. Useful as
a hedge, windbreak, or snow
trap in areas of extreme cold.
Flowers yellow and showy
in early spring.
height to 20 feet
zone 1 southward

Deutzia
Deutzia scabra

Double white flowers on drooping branches in May-June.
Most attractive when allowed to grow naturally.
height to 8 feet
zones 4 to 8

Dwarf ninebark
Physocarpus opulifolius nanus

A dwarf, compact, rounded shrub. White flowers in
clusters, small green foliage. An excellent hedge.
height to 3 feet
zones 3 to 9

Weeping forsythia
Forsythia suspensa

One of the most popular and unique
hedge plants. Large and bushy. it is easily
grown in sunny exposures. Branches arched
and in spring are smothered with
golden flowers.
height to 12 feet
zones 5 to 8

Golden vicary (Chartreuse shrub)

Ligustrum vicaryi

Distinctive golden yellow foliage that provides interesting contrast. A neat, compact shrub that can be clipped to any shape or height desired. It is a unique plant for borders. Best color in sun.

height to 6 feet
zones 5 to 9

Lodense privet

Ligustrum vulgare nanum

A low-growing privet that seldom needs shearing. Very hardy and ideally suited where a low hedge is desired. The nondwarf common privet (*Ligustrum vulgare*) can be used where taller hedging is desired.

height to 2-1/2 feet
zones 5 to 9

Dwarf privet

Ligustrum ovalifolium nanum

Low-growing form of America's most widely planted hedge. Semievergreen with thick, dark green foliage. Makes a dense, compact green wall.

height to 3 feet
zones 6 to 9

Lavender cotton

Santolina chamaecyparissus

Distinctive, silver-gray evergreen foliage. Yellow, globed flowers in June. Perfect for a low hedge. Not hardy north of zone 6 unless covered with straw mulch or with a cold frame.

height to 20 inches
zone 6 southward

Persian lilac

Syringa persica

One of the loveliest plants for tall hedges and screens. Its arching branches carry very fragrant, pale purple flowers in loose, broad clusters. Blooms in late spring.
height to 8 feet
zones 5 to 8

Japanese flowering quince

Chaenomeles lagenaria

The best flowering quince for use as hedging. Brilliant scarlet flowers appear before the foliage.
height to 6 feet
zones 5 to 9

Pekin cotoneaster

Cotoneaster acutifolia

Clusters of small pink flowers appear early in June, followed by black fruits that last almost through winter. The leaves are dark and glossy. Hardy and thrives even in poor, dry soils.
height to 12 feet
zones 4 to 9

Cranberry cotoneaster

Cotoneaster apiculata

An outstanding low hedge plant. During late summer and early fall its arching branches are covered with brilliant red fruit the size of cranberries. Shiny green foliage is semievergreen in cold climates.
height to 2 feet
zones 5 to 9

Spreading cotoneaster
Cotoneaster divaricata

A semievergreen with glossy dark foliage on arching branches. Heavy crops of bright red berries in fall. Holds foliage until late fall and is perhaps one of the easiest cotoneasters to grow.
height to 7 feet
zones 5 to 9

Abelia
Abelia grandiflora

A semievergreen with small, lustrous leaves that remain on most of the winter. Loose flower clusters of bluish white from late May until frost.
height to 5 feet
zone 6 southward

Midget hedge (Germander)
Teucrium chamaedrys

A low-growing hedge suitable for edging or in front of a wall. Resembles dwarf boxwood. It holds its leaves for 10 months of the year.
height to 15 inches
zones 5 to 8

Russian olive
Elaeagnus angustifolia

Silvery appearance due to coloring underneath foliage. Useful as windbreak or hedge, even in dry locations. Greenish flowers in June.
height to 20 feet
zone 3 southward

Dwarf arctic willow

Salix purpurea nana

A charming, low-growing willow excellent for low hedges. Grows in wet or heavy soils where other plants perish. Young twigs have purple color, foliage blue-green. Can be clipped to 12 inches high.
height to 3 feet
zones 5 to 8

Alpine currant

Ribes alpinum

Compact and upright habit. Grows fairly well in heavy shade and holds the dark green foliage until late fall. Can be trimmed as low as 12 inches. In early spring there are greenish yellow flowers followed by scarlet fruit.
height to 8 feet
zone 5 northward

Japanese barberry (Truehedge columnberry)

Berberis thunbergi erecta

Grows absolutely upright. Waxen, gleaming foliage turns to brilliant flame in autumn. Bright red berries remain all winter. Can be kept to 2 to 3 feet tall with one clipping a year.
height to 4 feet
zones 3 to 9

Amur maple

Acer ginnala

Beautiful foliage with reddish fruit. Fall foliage turns from brilliant orange to crimson. Easily trimmed for hedging.
height to 20 feet
zone 5 southward

Siberian elm

Ulmus pumila

Grows rapidly in the shade and does well in dry, poor soils as well as good soil. Will grow to tree height but can be sheared for very tall hedges or screening. Fall foliage red or purple in north but green southward.

height to 40 feet
zone 5 southward

Fragrant honeysuckle

Lonicera fragrantissima

A tall-growing hedge or screen. Not recommended where it is to be under 3 to 4 feet. Strong and vigorous, it is a dense grower and holds its foliage well into winter. Small, creamy bell-shaped blossoms in early spring. Red berries attract birds.

height to 12 feet
zones 6 to 9

VanHoutte spirea

Spirea vanhouttei

One of the most popular plants for use as a shrub. When allowed to grow naturally makes a beautiful screen or hedge. Withstands adverse conditions. Blooms profusely in May and June. Flowers are pure white and numerous on pendulous branches.

height to 6 feet
zone 4 southward

Winged euonymus

Euonymus alatus

While most often used as a specimen plant because of its fiery red color, winged euonymus also works well as a hedge. Dense branching habit provides uniformity. Winged branches add interest during winter months when leaves have fallen. Thrives in any soil under most varying exposures.

height to 9 feet
zones 5 to 9

Chinese photinia

Photinia serrulata

An evergreen shrub that can be sheared to desired height. It has deep green, glossy foliage and a dense, branching habit. The foliage colors brilliantly in the fall, and the small flowers produced in June are followed by red berries that are favored by birds.

heights to 40 feet
zones 7 to 9

Cherry laurel

Laurocerasus caroliniana

A handsome evergreen that can be grown into a tree or pruned to a hedge. Has dark, shiny green leaves and will become more compact each time it is sheared.

height to 40 feet
zones 8 to 9

English laurel
Laurocerasus officinalis

Large, dark green leaves resembling magnolia grandiflora.
Useful in foundation plantings and evergreen borders.
Not generally hardy north of Virginia.
height to 20 feet
zones 7 to 9

Zabel laurel
Laurocerasus officinalis zabeliana

An evergreen shrub with glossy foliage.
Fragrant white flowers and dark purple fruit.
Hardier than the English laurels but will
sometimes freeze north of zone 7.
height to 20 feet
zones 7 to 9

Burford holly
Ilex cornuta 'Burfordi'

Bright green foliage the year around
with a plentiful supply of big, bright
red berries in winter. Best planted in
protected places.
height to 10 feet
zones 7 to 9

Boxwood
Buxus

Long-lived, medium grower, and neat appearance throughout
the year. There are many varieties in this family
of broadleaved evergreens. Good for hedges and
topiary work.
height 3 to 25 feet
zones 5 to 9

arbor-vitae
boxwood
english laurel
hemlock
holly

Canadian or American hemlock

Tsuga canadensis

A hardy evergreen adapted to a wide range of soils. The foliage is dark green and lacy. Always graceful, sheared or unsheared. The best large evergreen for hedging.

height to 25 feet
zones 3 to 9

Arbor-vitae

Thuja

Variety of forms, rich foliar color, and hardiness have made arbor-vitae a standby for gardeners. Best grown in cool, moist locations. As hedging, effective sheared or natural. Pyramidal varieties are especially striking as hedges. Zones vary widely. Check with a local nurseryman for the variety that grows best in your area.

height varies
zones 3 to 9

Junipers
Juniperus

A large number of evergreen trees and shrubs are included in this pine family. Plants vary from low, prostrate shrubs to tall, narrow trees. They have either needle or scale foliage ranging in color from green to blue. The plants are valuable for their decorative characteristics and year-round color. Junipers lend themselves to natural-form edgings, borders, and hedges.
height varies
zone 4 southward

hedges

juniper
yew

Yews

Taxus

A number of varieties in the yew family lend themselves to hardy hedges and screens. The dark, rich green foliage makes an elegant hedge year-round. Should be pruned every summer to thicken and form shape. Among the best for hedges are the upright forms Hatfield, Hick's, and Hallaran.

height varies
zones 5 to 8

Hick's yew

Taxus media 'Hicks'

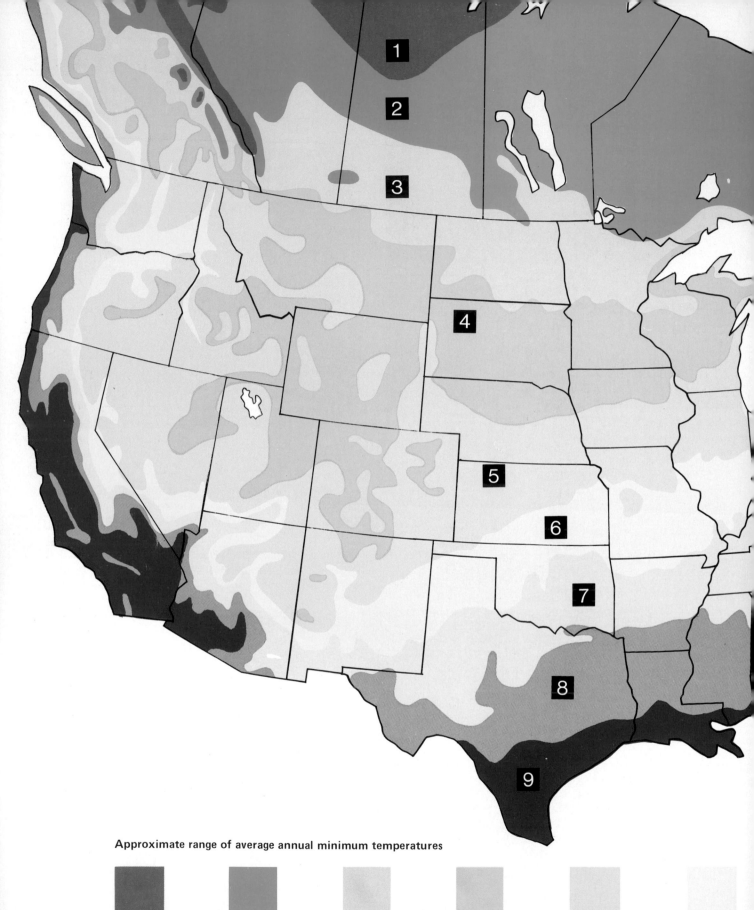

Approximate range of average annual minimum temperatures

zone **1** below −50°F	zone **2** −50° to −40°	zone **3** −40° to −30°	zone **4** −30° to −20°	zone **5** −20° to −10°	zone **6** −10° to 0°

This section of *Home Landscaping* brings together some detailed information you may need to plan and maintain your home landscape.

The **plant hardiness zone map** at the left shows the zones referred to in each plant listing in this book. If you want to design benches, tables, walks—or a driveway for easy car maneuvering—the section on **dimensions** will help.

There's a section on **planting** and another on **maintenance**. And if a plant starts to send distress signals, there's a section on **problems**, which will help you recognize those distress signals and tell you what you can do to help.

There are **lists** that show what plants to select for specific purposes and locations, a list of books, and a list of arboretums and public gardens.

Then, there's a **glossary** of terms related to plant materials and, finally, two **indexes**—one of common plant names, the other of their scientific names.

plant hardiness zones

e **7**
to 10°

zone **8**
10° to 20°

zone **9**
20° to 30°

zone **10**
30° to 40°

drives

scale: $\frac{1}{16}'' = 1'0''$

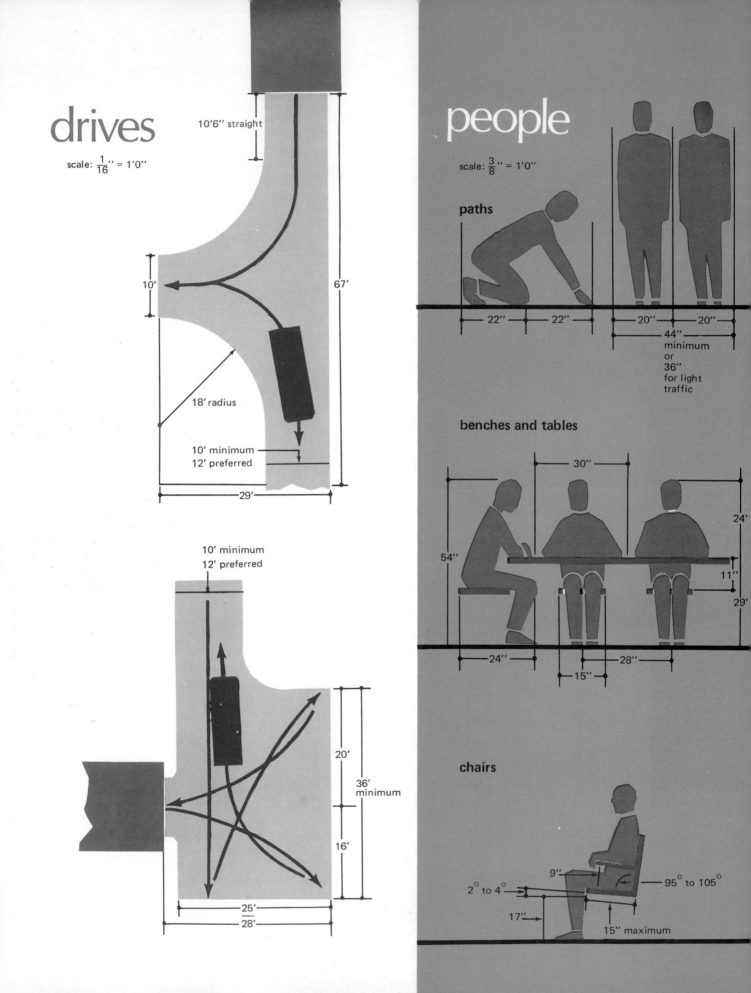

10'6'' straight

67'

10'

18' radius

10' minimum
12' preferred

29'

10' minimum
12' preferred

20'

36'
minimum

16'

25'
28'

people

scale: $\frac{3}{8}'' = 1'0''$

paths

22''   22''   20''   20''

44''
minimum
or
36''
for light
traffic

benches and tables

30''

54''   24''   11''   29''

24''   28''   15''

chairs

9''   95° to 105°

2° to 4°

17''   15'' maximum

plants

walks

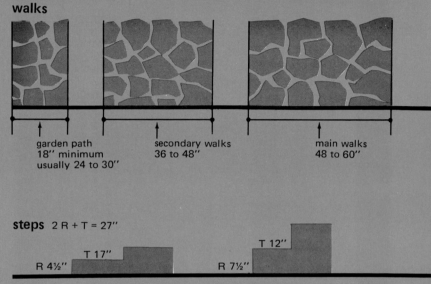

garden path
18" minimum
usually 24 to 30"

secondary walks
36 to 48"

main walks
48 to 60"

steps 2 R + T = 27"

R 4½"   T 17"

T 12"

R 7½"

leisurely rise

normal rise

patios

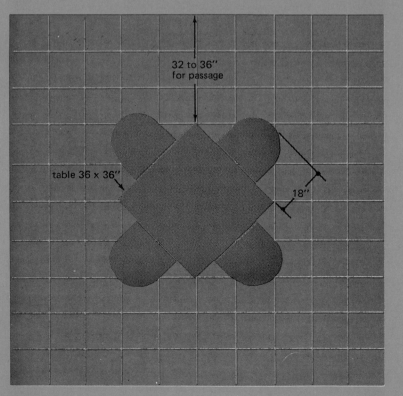

32 to 36"
for passage

table 36 x 36"

18"

planting distances

	Distance apart inches	Plants per sq. yard
Shrubs		
Dwarf & slow growing	18-24"	2-4
Medium	36-48"	1
Vigorous	60-72"	2-3
Bush roses	18-24"	3-4
Perennials		
Average	18-18"	4-9
Vigorous	24-48"	1-3
Small & ground cover	8-12"	9-25

trees height to spread ratios

	Height	Spread
Norway maple	5	4
Acer rubra	1	1
Sugar maple	4	3
Ginkgo	3	2
Thornless honey locust	3	2
Lombardy poplar	4	1
White oak Red oak	1	1
Pin oak	2	1
Weeping willow	5	4
Cornus florida	4	5
Japanese maple	1	1
Saucer magnolia	1	1
Malus	4	5

before planting

Be sure that plants and planting sites are compatible. Check with your local nurseryman about plant characteristics, such as affinity for sun or shade and wet or dry soil conditions. Also ask about the condition or the soil — whether it is predominantly wet or dry, acid or alkaline (its pH), and rich or poor in available nutrients. Nutrient deficiency, pH, and drainage problems should be corrected before planting.

Soil used in planting should be high in organic matter for better drainage and plant nutrition. This may be rich topsoil originally removed from the planting hole, original topsoil conditioned by the addition of one-third peat moss, or a commercially prepared topsoil and peat moss mixture. Chemical fertilizers may be added to correct for many nutrient deficiencies.

In heavy clay soil, provide drainage of the planting hole by digging or boring through the clay at the bottom of the hole. If such digging is not possible, dig a trench from the base of the planting hole laterally to drain at a point downslope. Put tile or stone in the drain.

Plants from the nursery come in various containers, each designed to keep roots moist until the time the plant goes into the ground. Balled and burlapped stock is packed with roots embedded in a ball of the soil in which it was grown, a method that minimizes shock of transplanting. Bare-rooted stock is packed in moisture-retaining material and bagged in paper or plastic. Packaging is removed just before planting.

Plants may also be potted in metal, plastic, or papier mache. Burlap and papier mache will deteriorate in the ground and need not be removed before planting, although ties around burlap bags should be removed and holes should be cut in papier mache containers. Plants that are packed or potted in plastic bags, metal or plastic pots must never be placed in the ground without removing the container.

balled and burlapped
Remove ties before planting. Burlap will rot in ground.

bare-rooted
Remove all packaging material just before planting.

container-grown
Cut holes in papier mache pot before planting. Discard metal or plastic containers.

Trees 5 feet or less need single stake secured to trunk with soft fabric or rubber hose-wrapped wire.

Trees over 5 feet may need stakes on opposite sides of trunk. Loosen ties occasionally.

Large trees subject to high winds need guys at several angles. Wind wires around pieces of board. Bury boards in ground.

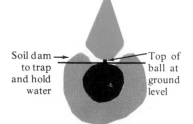

Soil dam to trap and hold water

Top of ball at ground level

Old soil mark at ground level

Soil dam to trap and hold water

Roots spread out, no crowding. Soil packed firmly with no air pockets.

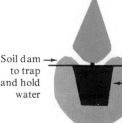

Soil dam to trap and hold water

Papier mache pot with holes cut in it. Never plant metal or plastic container.

trees

balled and burlapped

1. Dig a hole deeper than the height of the ball and wide enough to allow 6 inches between bag and sidewalls all around.
2. Provide drainage in heavy clay soil.
3. Spade bottom of hole well and thoroughly mix in peat moss, leaf mold, or vermiculite and enough topsoil to bring top of ball to ground level.
4. Place tree in completed hole, handling plant by the ball only.
5. Force garden hose to bottom of hole. Begin filling hole with soil, firming it down gradually to eliminate air pockets. Slowly let hole fill with water.
6. Backfill to top of ball with soil high in organic matter, which will promote better drainage and provide nutrients for the tree's root system.
7. After water has disappeared from surface, finish filling hole until soil reaches original ground level. Do not mound. Grade soil so that water drains toward trunk. Form a small dam around perimeter of area. The soil will gradually settle, creating a depression to trap moisture.
8. Prune broken and damaged branches. In general, thin all trees except evergreens to reduce excessive loss of moisture before root system is established.
9. Mulch the planting area with a heavy layer or organic matter.
10. Wrap all smooth-barked trees that are subject to sunscald.
11. Protect young trees from rabbit damage by wrapping hardware cloth around trunk to a height of 24 to 30 inches.

bare-rooted

Site preparation and planting are the same as those for balled and burlapped trees, with these exceptions:
1. Make hole wide enough to accommodate roots without crowding and deep enough to plant tree to its original depth.
2. Remove all packaging materi$ls from around the roots, and trim off broken root ends.
3. Lay out roots in natural position on pack-down topsoil at bottom of hole.
4. Straighten and stake the tree. Trees 4 feet or less require a single stake driven several inches from trunk. Larger trees may require two or more stakes. The trunk is tied to the stake with soft fabric or pieces of rubber hose. Ties should be loosened occasionally so that bark is not injured.
5. Work soil in carefully around roots, eliminating all air pockets as filling and watering proceed.

shrubs

balled and burlapped

1. Dig hole wide enough to allow 6 inches between ball and sidewalls and deeper than height of ball.
2. Fill hole with enough soil to bring top of ball to ground level.
3. Tamp soil and set shrub in hole, handling plant by the ball only.
4. Remove all strings tied around trunk.
5. Fill hole to top of ball.
6. Plunge hose nozzle deep into root zone and fill with water.
7. After water settles away, finish filling to ground level. Form a soil dam around perimeter of area.
8. Mulch area with organic material.

bare-rooted

1. Dig hole 1 1/2 times depth of root mass and about twice width of plant. Partly fill hole with soil.
2. Remove all packaging materials from around the roots, and cut off broken or damaged roots.
3. Place shrub in hole so that crown or graft is at ground level.
4. Fill hole to ground level, working soil in carefully around roots and packing it down.
5. Sink hose nozzle into root zone and water until surface is flooded.
6. After water settles away, add soil to ground level and form soil dam around perimeter of area.
7. Mulch area with organic material.

container-grown

1. Dig hole several inches deeper than container, allowing plenty of width for root growth.
2. Loosen soil at bottom of hole. Remove plant from container, soil and all, or cut holes in papier mache pot. Set plant with enough soil beneath to bring crown or graft to ground level.
3. Fill hole to ground level and water thoroughly.
4. After water subsides, tamp soil, add more soil, and form soil dam around perimeter of area.
5. Mulch area with organic material.

ground covers, hedges

ground covers

Soil requirements for ground covers vary. Plant shallow-rooted types in easily crumbled soil so that they will be less susceptible to winter freezing, thawing, and other root stresses.

Small ground cover plants, including most perennials and low shrubs, such as euonymus, Japanese spurge, and myrtle, should be spaced from 6 to 12 inches apart depending on species and size of plants.

Large, woody plants , such as boxwood, bittersweet, and needled evergreens, should be planted much farther apart. However, if ground cover plants are placed too far apart, the ground between may erode or fill with weeds before plants grow together.

hedges

Hedges that drop their leaves can be planted in spring or fall. Evergreen hedges should be planted in early spring. Set hedge plants a little lower than they were in nursery to get a dense hedge at bottom.

Set all small plants, except evergreens, a foot apart. The smallest hedges, such as privet, may be set closer. Large plants are set farther apart, either in a trench or in individual holes.

To be assured of a straight hedge, stretch a string between two stakes over the proposed planting area, or dig one side of trench straight and in line and place plants against straight side. Visually line up any plants that are not symmetrically balanced.

All hedges, except evergreens, should be severely cut back at planting to encourage bushing from the base and to reduce excessive loss of water while plants are establishing root systems.

hedges

For more bottom growth, set plants with crown or graft slightly lower than old soil mark.

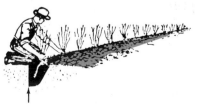

To set hedge straight, stand plants against side of trench dug straight down and in line.

pruning

Homeowners prune deciduous and evergreen trees and shrubs for the following reasons.

1. To remove dead or dying branches due to storms, winterkill, or disease.
2. To help young stock develop proper structure for supporting future growth, including removal of crossed branches that rub and bruise other branches.
3. To keep shape and size compatible with landscaping scheme.
4. To stimulate increased flower and fruit production.
5. To bring old overgrown plants back to manageable dimensions.
6. To balance foliage with available root system during the transplanting process.

trees

Trees are usually trimmed to remove dead or damaged limbs, to curtail competition between limbs growing too close together, and to influence structure.

This work is usually done in early spring, although most species can be pruned almost any time. Exceptions are trees that bleed profusely, such as maples. Such trees should be pruned when growing actively rather than during dormancy.

Dead or dying limbs should be cut off flush with the nearest living limb. This same rule applies to two competing limbs originating from the same point on the crown. These are called double leaders and are subject to damage by strong winds or, in the case of fruit trees, damage by a too bountiful harvest. Cut out the poorer leader.

When you cannot reach limbs to be pruned, call a tree surgeon.

Pruning deciduous trees when first planted or cutting back old deciduous trees when transplanted is beneficial. Growth above the ground is balanced with the amount of root system remaining to sustain life. This pruning will also improve structural strength. The structure should complement the original form or shape that characterizes that particular species.

The beauty of many trees is destroyed by pruning away the lower branches to allow for easier mowing. Shade trees like elms, maples, locusts, and sycamores may be pruned without destruction of form to allow mowing under them. Crabs, hawthorns, beeches, amur maples, plums and other ornamentals* should be allowed to assume their natural forms. Mowing beneath them should be discontinued when the branches become larger. Mulches or ground covers established under such trees eliminate grass and the need for subsequent mowing.

The primary way to encourage high branching in newly planted, young shade trees is to remove some of the lower limbs each year for several years. Don't remove all low limbs. The plant needs the foliage to carry on life processes.

Suckers that begin near the base of the plant, farther up the trunk, and between branches should be cut off at first appearance.

deciduous shrubs

Buds on deciduous stem ends are called terminal and elongate the stem. Buds along the length of the stem are called lateral and form leaves and branches. When the terminal buds are cut off, the lateral bud closest to the cut is stimulated to accelerated growth.

This phenomenon helps gardeners influence shrub shape. When a shrub needs denser inside foliage, branches should be trimmed back to the lateral bud growing toward the shrub's interior.

When a plant is too erect or too dense, cut back stems to an outside lateral bud to achieve a more open effect. When a dense top is wanted, branch ends should be trimmed back to stimulate growth from the lateral buds.

To remove dead growth, cut back to the nearest living lateral branch growing in the direction desired. It may, at times, be necessary to remove a branch at ground level.

When large flowers are desired on shrubs, such as hydrangeas, a severe heading back (trimming at the top) will stimulate larger but fewer blooms.

Severe pruning is also necessary for rejuvenating an old plant. Some old plants have many limbs arising from the ground.

Carefully cut out one-third of the oldest branches. Preserve as much symmetry as possible. Trim back the remaining branches as needed to shape the shrub.

Next year remove an additional one-third of the old stems. Be sure to retain the new growth that resulted from the previous year's pruning. After all of the old wood is removed, the shrub should consist of new, vigorous, growing stems. Select the most vigorous and remove the unwanted branches. Some pruning to shape the new growth may be necessary.

In extremely rapid-growing shrubs, such as honeysuckles, rejuvenation is best accomplished by removing all of the top growth at one time, encouraging new growth from the base.

When a shrub grows out of bounds, it may be improved by thinning out dead, weak, or overcrowded branches.

When selecting shrubs, especially for foundation plantings, consider their ultimate height and general form. With wise selection, drastic pruning may never be necessary.

As with trees, it is necessary when planting deciduous shrubs to prune back foliage to balance the root system.

In general, all deciduous shrubs fall into two classes for pruning purposes — those that should be pruned immediately after flowering and those that should be pruned in the early spring. The first class forms its flowers on the previous year's growth and the second on the current year's growth. The first class is composed of early bloomers and the latter are late summer and fall bloomers. Examples of each are listed here.

Pruned in early spring
Anthony Waterer
  spirea   Hydrangea
Butterfly bush   Rose of Sharon
Douglas spirea

Pruned after flowering
Deutzia   Mockorange
Forsythia   Quince
Honeysuckle   Spirea
Lilac   Weigela

evergreen shrubs

Evergreens are frequently used when formal effects are desired because of their symmetry. Pruning in these instances should retain this symmetry.

Long shoots on previously shaped plants tend to destroy the original symmetry unless they are pruned annually. Annual pruning or shearing to head back such new growth will cause the plants to become dense and retain the desired symmetry.

Where low-spreading shrubs are needed, but shrubs of improper scale were selected, the form and scale can be retained by pruning off the rapid-growing side and top branches. Formalized cone-shaped forms need to be discouraged from sending out spreading branches that erase the original intended shape. Such growth cannot be stopped, so annual pruning becomes necessary.

Most evergreens can be pruned almost any time. Pines, however, should be pruned during the period of new growth. Pruning should be avoided late in the growing season to avoid stimulating new growth that would have difficulty hardening off before heavy frosts occur.

Pruning storm damage can be done any time.

It should be noted that all plants look best as nature intended them. Shrubs of proper scale, rate of growth, and density should require little or no pruning. Formal designs, on the other hand, often require extensive pruning to restrain growth patterns.

ground covers

Pruning ground covers until the plants have grown together will encourage growth and create stronger, more compact plants. When you use various ground covers near one another, careful study should be made to insure harmonious relationships of line patterns and pleasing compositions of texture, color, and mass.

hedges

Clip a hedge before it becomes too tall. Cut it back two or three times the first season. This will tend to force growth at the base and develop a thicker hedge. Development of branches at the base is also encouraged by trimming the hedge narrower at the top than at the bottom. This allows sunlight to reach the entire lower part of the plant uniformly.

Hedges are normally used for formal effects or where space is limited. If the same kind of effect can be achieved with informal plantings, avoid formal hedges, which require greater maintenance. Slow-growing plants may take more time to reach desired size, but they require many fewer clippings during the year.

food and water

Fertilizer plays an important part in the development of horticultural plantings. Frequent light applications promote better color and vigor and faster rates of growth than do heavy doses once or twice a year. But, as with so many chemicals, it is best to check with a professional before applying fertilizer.

Lawn fertilizer will not always be the proper mixture for trees and shrubs. This is particularly critical in certain areas such as the South and Far West where severe mineral imbalances are encountered and micronutrients* are required.

The debate continues over which fertilizer is better, organic or inorganic*. Agronomists say both are needed for optimum growth.

Inorganic fertilizers are guaranteed by grade to deliver specific nutrients in specific amounts. A high percentage of water solubility is a reliable indicator of the fertilizer's worth. The grower always knows the amount of each nutrient that will be available to the plant.

Organic materials are not reliable in their available nutrient content. How many pounds of nitrogen are there in a bushel of leaves? It all depends.

Organic materials do help preserve rainfall and, when worked into the soil, provide pore spaces for air and water. Beneficial soil microbe activity is increased by organic matter. Breakdown of organic matter releases additional amounts of nitrogen, phosphorus, and potassium, which are major growth elements.

Water is both a nutrient and a carrier of nutrients. To increase the moisture-holding capacity of the soil, cultivate the ground around plants to create a dust mulch*.

All shrubs and trees need periodic waterings. Where dry winters occur and drying winds are common, it is necessary to water in early spring. Ample waterings in late fall will help trees and shrubs, particularly evergreens, get through the winter in good health.

During dry summer months evergreens should be watered thoroughly, particularly during the first year. Do not spray the plant; instead, soak the soil around the plant's base.

planting, maintenance

Transplanting shock commonly occurs when trees or shrubs are moved while they are partly or fully leafed out. Shock also may occur if roots are excessively pruned or the ball is dug too small during transplanting, even if the plant is dormant.

The use of antidesiccants on new foliage helps reduce the loss of water and aids successful transplanting. When it becomes impossible to transplant at the recommended time, dig larger than normal-sized balls to take a greater number of roots.

Planting too deeply is a common reason for poor growth of many shrubs, including azaleas, camellias, boxwood, dogwood, yews, and pines.

Check to see if lower limbs of the plant are covered with soil. Also dig around the base of the plant to determine if the crown is too far below the soil level. If you find the plant has been set too deeply, remove it in early spring while it is dormant, add a soil-organic matter mix to the bottom of the hole, and replant.

Overfertilization with an inorganic fertilizer is a very common reason for sudden leaf drop or dying of some shrubs during the growing season. Dying of the tips or borders of leaves can be a symptom of fertilizer injury to the root system.

Water affected plants heavily a few times to leach excess fertilizer out of the root zone. After this, keep plants well watered during the recovery period when new roots are forming.

Improper pruning with hedge shears may remove most tip growth and future flower buds. Berry-producing plants are best pruned by removal of individual limbs inside the plant.

soil, drainage

Poor soil preparation often occurs in areas where soil has been compacted by heavy construction equipment and stripped of topsoil. These areas need organic matter incorporated in the soil before planting and mulch to insure a suitable base for drainage and root expansion.

Work in a form of organic matter with existing soils before planting. Dig a large hole so that the root system can penetrate into the new soil mix. Good sources of organic matter are peat moss, peat humus, rotted leaf mold, well-rotted manure, partly decomposed sawdust, partly rotted material from compost piles, and cereal straw. Apply extra nitrogen during the first growing season if sawdust or cereal straw is added as organic matter.

If plants have been planted in extremely poor soil, dig them up during dormancy in the early spring and make proper soil preparations before replanting.

Improper soil pH, the degree of acidity or alkalinity of a soil, is often referred to as its sweetness or sourness. This soil condition is reflected in the loss of vigor accompanied by yellowing or other discoloration of foliage.

Have soil tested. If yellowing occurs because of excessive alkalinity, apply chelated iron, ferrous sulfate, or zinc sulfate to the surrounding soil. This action is temporary and repeated applications may be warranted if the symptoms return. Agricultural lime will modify most acid problems.

Nutritional deficiency is a foremost cause of yellowing foliage.

Nitrogen deficiency usually shows up in lower foliage first and causes an even, light green color. Iron and zinc deficiencies are most prevalent in extremely alkaline soil and where construction mortar is in the soil.

Iron chlorosis causes yellowing of the youngest foliage in a definite pattern. Leaf veins usually remain green while the areas between veins become yellow-green to yellow.

Correct nitrogen deficiency by adding recommended amounts of nitrogen fertilizer around the base of the plant within the drip line. Then add enough water to move fertilizer into the root zone.

Zinc and iron chlorosis can be corrected by adding iron or zinc sulfate or chelates to the soil or by spraying a solution on the plant itself. Foliar spraying, however, is a short-term solution and must be done often to keep the plant in good health.

Pool soil drainage is common in heavy clay soil and extremely evident where the soil is compacted.

Depressions in the yard surface and excess water at a downspout or other drain tile may contribute to poor drainage.

Divert drain spouts past plants. If a plant is located in a depressed area, remove it, increase the soil level so that water will not accumulate in the area, then replant at the new level. Do not attempt to fill in around the plant to correct the soil depression. In dense clay soil, tile or fill planting hole with coarse gravel to facilitate drainage.

Excess soil drainage occurs when plants are located in a gravelly area or in fill material containing large rocks.

Remove perennial plants and replace with annual ornamentals. If removal is impractical, apply water more frequently to the area. Since added water will result in a more rapid leaching of available nitrogen, make additional nitrogen applications during the growing season.

weather, accidents

Frost or cold damage to stems often results in bark splitting or death of buds and tender growth. This condition may not become evident until spring or summer. If only certain limbs are affected, examine them for dieback and split bark.

Cold damage to leaves often occurs in early spring after leaf buds have swollen but leaves have not emerged. The damage usually is not visible until a month or more later. It is characterized by such malformations of the leaves as puckering, twisting or curling. The affected leaves are small when compared with leaves that emerge later.

Cold damage during the flowering period most often accounts for failure to produce berries. However, failure to produce fruit may also be the result of the plant's sex. Male plants produce no berries, and female plants will produce no berries in the absence of a male plant to fertilize them.

Sunscald can occur during the winter as well as the summer, particularly when trees and shrubs are subjected to a southwest exposure of bright sunlight. The reflection of sun on snow can increase stem temperatures and cause sap to flow. A rapid decrease in temperature then can cause stem damage similar to that caused by cold damage. The bark will appear to be scalded and will eventually dry out and loosen from the trunk.

Protect the trunk from winter and summer sunscald by wrapping with a tree-wrap paper, burlap, or other material that shades the trunk.

Drought damage is likely to occur in plants set in poorly prepared soil. Lack of water also is a primary reason for the death of many recently transplanted woody ornamentals. When needed, water the soil around the base of new plants thoroughly during the first year.

Heat damage may occur when plants are situated near a white building or fence, or when extensive white stone mulches are used. The reflection of the sun's rays intensifies the heat in the immediate vicinity of the foliage. The leaf tips, margins, or the entire leaf may suddenly dry and turn brown.

Apply more water to the plant, move the location of the plant, repaint the structure, or replace stone mulch with a different kind to reduce heat reflection.

Lawnmower damage results in stunted growth or sudden death of shrubs and small trees located in the lawn area. If the trunk is completely girdled, the plant will die.

Lawnmower damage can be prevented by exercising care to avoid mechanical contact with the plant. Hand trim or remove a circle of sod around the base of the plant. Replace sod with a ground cover. All tree wounds should be dressed.

Gas injury to plants can occur as the result of gas leakage. Trees, shrubs, and grass may suddenly die. All plant life in the leakage area is usually affected, not just one or two plants.

pests, diseases

Root rots or *insects* attacking the root system are likely suspects if plants lose vigor and die. Such injury is difficult to correct. Eliminate as many stresses as possible and stimulate new root growth by proper watering and fertilization. Professional help may be needed to control insects.

Borer damage causes foliage to die, particularly on shrubs and trees, such as dogwood, birch, lilac, mountain ash, and Scotch pine. Check the trunk for borer holes, oozing sap, bits of sawdust, or dead bark. Extract the borer, then paint all wounds with a wound compound.

Animal girdling by mice and rabbits is a frequent problem with new plantings and in areas where animal forage is sparse. Damage results from animals gnawing the bark near the plant's base and occasionally higher during periods of snow accumulation.

Encircle the base of the plant with hardware cloth or heavy roofing paper to a height of 2 to 3 feet. Euonymus, crab, cotoneaster, and shadblow are the most frequently attacked plantings.

Cat damage in the form of partial or complete girdling can occur if these animals sharpen their claws on the trunks of young trees. Wrap finely woven wire around the trunk to a height of 2 to 3 feet. The wire can be held in place by weaving stakes through the wire and pushing them into the soil.

Floral diseases attacking developing flowers may kill the buds before they open. When mild attacks occur, the flower may be discolored or deformed. Floral diseases may also attack developing berries and fruits.

To reduce incidence of floral disease, improve air circulation by pruning excess branches. This opens the canopy of the plant, allowing more rapid drying of the foliage during periods of wet weather. When watering the plant, confine the stream to the base of the plant.

lists

The lists that follow will help you choose plant materials for a variety of different purposes.

Want shade trees or ornamental plantings? Consult the lists of trees that are best for providing shade and trees and shrubs to plant to show off shapes, colors, and flowers. What plants will be best near your patio or in that somewhat cramped space between your driveway and your neighbor's property line? There are lists of plants for these places. And there are lists of plants that will thrive in those problem areas where the soil is always just a little too wet—or dry or sandy or erosion-prone.

A list of plants and the months in which they bloom shows you what to plant for floral beauty from March through October—and for decorative fruit, twigs, or bark that can be enjoyed the year round.

Ground covers and vines can be chosen for problem areas, for flowers, for leaf colors. These lists will help you pick the best plants for a particular purpose. Do you want a formal, clipped hedge or an informal, let-it-do-its-own-thing hedge? There are lists of plants that are best for either style.

If you want to visit a public garden or arboretum, check the list on page 139. Even if there aren't any close to your home, perhaps you'll find one that you can visit on a vacation trip.

Finally, has this book whetted your appetite for more knowledge of the subject of landscaping? If it has, there's a short list of books on the subject on page 139. Not a complete list—we'd need to print another book for that. But enough to help you decide if you want to dig deeper (no pun intended) than you already have.

trees

specimen deciduous trees
Alder, European
Ash, European mountain
Birch, clump
Crab, Beverly
Crab, Japanese zumi
Crab, midget
Crab, prairie
Crab, purple
Crab, Sargent
Crab, Van Eseltine
Dogwood, flowering
Dogwood, pagoda
Fringe-tree, white
Ginkgo
Golden rain tree
Gum, sweet
Hawthorn, dotted
Hawthorn, Lavalle
Hawthorn, Washington
Hawthorn, Winterking
Lilac, Japanese tree
Linden, American
Linden, Greenspire littleleaf
Linden, Redmond
Locust, thornless
Magnolia, saucer
Maple, Amur
Maple, Japanese
Maple, Norway
Maple, red
Maple, sugar
Mountain ash
Oak, burr
Oak, pin
Oak, red
Oak, scarlet
Oak, white
Olive, Russian
Photinia, oriental
Redbud, Eastern
Serviceberry
Tulip tree
Yellowwood

specimen evergreen trees
Arbor-vitae, Little Gem
Cedar, Atlas
Cryptomeria, Lobb
Cypress, dwarf hinoki
Cypress, hinoki
Cypress, Lawson
Cypress, Sawara
Fir, concolor
Fir, Douglas
Fir, Fraser
Fir, Nikko
Fir, pyramidal Douglas
Hemlock, Canadian
Hemlock, Carolina
Pine, Austrian
Pine, Japanese table
Pine, Japanese white
Pine, limber
Pine, red
Pine, Scotch
Pine, sentinel
Pine, Swiss stone
Pine, weeping white
Pine, white
Spruce, Black Hills
Spruce, Colorado
Spruce, dwarf Alberta
Spruce, Norway
Spruce, oriental
Spruce, Serbian

trees for street planting
Ash, green
Ginkgo
Hackberry
Linden, Greenspire littleleaf
Locust, Moraine
Locust, Sunburst
Locust, thornless
Maple, Norway
Maple, Schwedler
Oak, pin

trees for screens and windbreaks
Beech, European
Cork-tree, Amur
Fir, Douglas
Hawthorn, cockspur
Hawthorn, Washington
Hemlock, Eastern
Hornbeam, European
Ironwood
Larch, European
Maple, Amur
Maple, hedge
Oak, pin
Olive, Russian
Pine, Austrian
Pine, red
Pine, Scotch
Pine, white
Poplar, Bolleana
Poplar, Lombardy
Spruce, Colorado
Spruce, Norway
Spruce, white

shrubs

trees for patios
Alder, European
Birch, river
Crab, Profusion
Dogwood, Cornelian cherry
Dogwood, flowering
Fringe-tree, white
Golden rain tree
Linden, European littleleaf
Magnolia, saucer
Maple, Japanese
Redbud
Serviceberry
Silverbell, Carolina
Yellowwood

trees for narrow areas
Crab, midget
Crab, tea
Hawthorn, Washington
Hornbeam, columnar
Maple, columnar Norway
Maple, columnar red
Oak, pyramidal

trees for shade
Ash, green
Birch, river
Buckeye, Ohio
Coffee-tree, Kentucky
Cork-tree, Amur
Ginkgo
Ironwood
Linden, American
Linden, littleleaf
Linden, Redmond
Locust, Sunburst
Locust, Moraine
Locust, thornless
Maple, Norway
Maple, red
Maple, Schwedler
Maple, sugar
Oak, burr
Oak, pin
Oak, red
Oak, white
Shadblow, Allegheny

trees for wet soil
Alder, European
Ash, white
Birch, river
Buckeye, Ohio
Hackberry
Linden, American
Magnolia, sweet bay
Maple, red
Maple, silver
Oak, pin
Oak, swamp white
Sycamore
Walnut, black
Willow

trees for fall brilliance
Buckeye, Ohio
Dogwood, flowering
Ginkgo
Gum, sour
Gum, sweet
Hawthorn, Washington
Hornbeam, American
Katsura tree
Maple, Amur
Maple, red
Maple, sugar
Oak, pin
Oak, scarlet
Pear, dwarf callery
Serviceberry

shrubs for lawn specimen, border, and screen planting

sunny locations

high growing
Beauty bush
Deutzia, Pride of Rochester
Dogwoods (various)
Elder, golden
Forsythia
Highbush cranberry
Honeysuckle, tatarian
Hydrangea, panicled
Jetbead
Lilac, Persian
Lilacs, French hybrid
Olive, Russian
Pussy willow
Rose acacia
Rose of Sharon
Snowball
Sumac, cutleaved
Tamarix
Weigelas (various)

medium and low growing
Almond, flowering
Barberry
Butterfly bush
Coralberry
Cotoneaster
Deutzia, Lemoine
Deutzia, slender
Dogwoods (various)
Hydrangea, snow hill
Kerria, Japanese
Mockorange
Privet, Regel's
Quince, flowering
Snowberry
Spirea, Anthony Waterer
Spirea, billiard
Spirea, plumleaf
Spirea, VanHoutte
Weigelas (various)

shady locations

high growing
Arrowwood
Deutzia, Pride of Rochester
Dogwoods (various)
Forsythia, Golden Bell
Highbush cranberry
Honeysuckles (various)
Mockoranges (various)
Nannyberry
Snowball
Tamarix
Viburnum, mapleleaf

medium and low growing
Barberry, Japanese
Coralberry
Currant, Indian
Elder, golden
Honeysuckle, winter
Hydrangea, panicled
Hydrangea, snow hill
Kerria, Japanese
Snowberry
Spirea, Anthony Waterer

shrubs for base planting

sunny locations

high growing
Bluebeard
Crape myrtle
Deutzia, Pride of Rochester
Dogwoods (various)
Honeysuckle, fragrant
Honeysuckle, pink
Mockorange
Pearl bush
Tamarix
Weigelas (various)

medium growing
Beauty-berry
Butterfly bush
Chokeberry
Coralberry
Cotoneasters (various)
Elder, golden
Hydrangeas (various)
Ninebark
Privet, Regel's
St. John's wort
Snowberry
Spireas (various)

shrubs *continued*

low growing

Barberry
Cinquefoil
Daphne
Kerria, Japanese
Spirea, Anthony Waterer
Spirea, Froebel

shady locations

high growing

Arrowwood
Dogwoods (various)
Highbush cranberry
Honeysuckle, tatarian
Nannyberry
Privet, Amur
Witch-hazel

medium growing

Cotoneaster
Currant, flowering
Dogwoods (various)
Elder, golden
Honeysuckle, winter
Hydrangea, snow hill
Jetbead
Privet, Regel's

low growing

Barberry
Cinquefoil
Coralberry
Currant, alpine
Kerria, Japanese
Snowberry
Stephanandra, cutleaf

planned plantings for all-season color

March

Daphne, Mezereon
  (lilac, purple)
Dogwood, Cornelian cherry
  (yellow)
Honeysuckle, fragrant
  (white)
Rhododendron
  (rosy purple)
Witch-hazel, vernal
  (reddish yellow)

April

Azalea, torch
  (orange to pale pink)
Cherry, Nanking
  (white)
Golden bells
  (yellow)
Pea tree, Siberian
  (yellow)
Quince, flowering
  (salmon-pink-red)
Quince, Japanese
  (scarlet red)
Spirea, garland
  (white)
Sumac, fragrant
  (yellow)
Viburnum, Burkwood
  (whitish pink)

May

Azaleas
  (orange to red)
Beauty bush
  (pink)
Chokeberry
  (white)
Cotoneaster
  (whitish pink)
Honeysuckle
  (purple, white, pink, yellow)
Jetbead
  (white)
Lilacs
  (lilac, purple, white)
Mockorange
  (white)
Viburnum, double file
  (white)
Wayfaring bush
  (white)
Weigelas
  (white, pink, crimson)

June

Cinquefoil
  (yellow)
Firethorn
  (white)
Hydrangea, oakleaf
  (white)
Hydrangea, snow hill
  (white)
Ninebark
  (white)
Privet, Amur
  (white)
Privet, Regel's
  (white)
St. John's wort
  (yellow)
Snowberry
  (pink)
Spirea, Anthony Waterer
  (crimson)
Spirea, Froebel
  (crimson)

July

Abelia, glossy
  (light pink)
Rose of Sharon
  (red, purple, white)
Sweet pepperbush
  (white)

August-September

Bluebeard
  (blue)

October

Witch-hazel
  (yellow)

shrubs with attractive late-season effects

decorative fruit

Arrowwood
Japanese barberry
Bayberry
Beauty-berry
Chokeberry
Coralberry
Cotoneaster (various)
Indian currant
Dogwoods (various)
Firethorn
Highbush cranberry
Winterberry holly
Honeysuckle
Nannyberry
Ninebark
Privet
Japanese snowball
Snowberry
Wayfaring bush

decorative twigs or bark

Winged burning bush
Cinquefoil
Dogwoods (various)
Forsythia (various)
Honeysuckle (various)
Jetbead
Japanese kerria
Ninebark
Quince
Garland spirea
Viburnums (various)

shrubs that yield brilliant fall coloring

Japanese barberry
Red leaf barberry
Dwarf burning bush
Winged burning bush
Hazelnut
Ninebark
Smoke tree
Sumac (various)
Viburnum (various)
Witch-hazel

lists

ground covers

shrubs with fruits that attract birds

Barberry
Bayberry
Buckthorn
Coralberry
Alpine currant
Indian currant
Dogwoods (various)
Elderberry
Honeysuckle (various)
St. John's wort
European privet
Dwarf shadblow
Snowberry
European spindle tree
Spirea (various)
Sumac (various)
Viburnums (various)
Weigela

shrubs for shady banks

Japanese barberry
Coralberry
Alpine currant
Indian currant
Arnold's dwarf forsythia
Honeysuckle (various)
Snowberry
Sumac (various)
Tamarix

shrubs that thrive in dry soils

Japanese barberry
Glossy buckthorn
Cinquefoil
Coralberry
Indian currant
Gray dogwood
Forsythia (various)
Honeysuckle (various)
Privet
Siberian pea tree
Snowberry
Billiard spirea
Fragrant sumac
Tamarix
Wayfaring bush

shrubs that thrive in wet soils

Alder
Arrowwood
Buttonbush
Chokeberry
Dogwoods (various)
Golden elder
Elderberry
Hardhack
Winterberry holly
Hydrangeas (various)
Nannyberry
Spicebush
Billiard spirea
Swamp rose
Willow

spreading evergreens

tall growing

Blue Pfitzer juniper
Hetz juniper
Meyer juniper
Savin juniper
Von Ehren juniper
Brown's yew
Japanese spreading yew

medium growing

Globe arbor-vitae
Golden Pfitzer juniper
Maney juniper
Dwarf mugo pine
Dwarf Japanese yew
Newport spreading yew
Serbian yew
Taunton spreading yew

upright evergreens

medium growing

Dark green arbor-vitae
Pyramidal arbor-vitae
Ames juniper
Burk juniper
Canaert juniper
Hillspire juniper
Iowa juniper
Spiny creek juniper
Welch juniper
Japanese upright yew

low growing

Blackman's golden arbor-vitae
Blue cone arbor-vitae
Holmstrup arbor-vitae
Tom Thumb arbor-vitae

columnar evergreens

Irish juniper
Halloran yew
Hatfield yew
Hick's yew

low-growing, creeping evergreens

Andorra juniper
Arcadia juniper
Arctic juniper
Blue rug juniper
Broadmoor juniper
Dwarf Japanese juniper
Hughes juniper
Japanese juniper
San Jose juniper
Sargent juniper
Tamarix juniper
Waukegan juniper
Yellow variegated juniper

herbaceous perennial ground covers

Artemisia
Bugle
Candytuft
Fescue, blue mist
Ginger, wild
Goutweed
Lace plant, dwarf
Lily-of-the-valley
Pachysandra
Phlox, creeping
Plantain-lily, whiterim blunt
Sedum
Thyme, creeping
Veronica

broadleaf evergreen ground covers

Bearberry
Boxwood, wintergreen
Euonymus, wintercreeper
Garland flower
Honeysuckle, Hall's
Ivy, Baltic
Lily turf
Myrtle
Pachysandra
Rat-stripper

deciduous ground covers

Bittersweet
Coralberry
Cotoneaster, rock
Forsythia, Arnold's dwarf
Forsythia, dwarf
Rose, memorial
St. John's wort

ground covers for shade and partial shade

Barberry, creeping
Bishop's weed
Bittersweet
Bugle
Bugleweed
Candytuft
Coralberry
Cotoneaster
Crown vetch
Euonymus, wintercreeper
Euonymus, small-leaved
Hemlock, ground
Honeysuckle, Hall's

ground covers *continued*

Ivy, Baltic
Ivy, English
Lily-of-the-valley
Moneywort
Myrtle
Navelwort
Oregon grape holly
Pachysandra
Plantain-lily
Rat-stripper
St. John's wort
Sand myrtle
Sedum
Silveredge
Thyme, creeping
Veronica
Viola

ground covers for sunny places

Artemisia
Barberry
Bearberry
Bishop's weed
Bluebell
Boxwood, Korean
Bugle
Candytuft
Cotoneaster, rock
Cottage pink
Crown vetch
Forsythia, dwarf
Garland flower
Honeysuckle
Houseleek
Lace plant, dwarf
Pachysandra
Phlox, creeping
Plantain-lily
Rat-stripper
Rose, memorial
Sedum
Snow-in-summer
Veronica
Viola

ground covers for moist soil

Forget-me-not
Galax
Lily-of-the-valley
Partridgeberry
Phlox
Plantain-lily
Sandwort, moss
Siberian tea
Star violet
Swamp dewberry
Wild Sweet William
Wintergreen

ground covers for dry soil

Artemisia
Bearberry
Crown vetch
Houseleek
Phlox
Rat-stripper
Sedum
Thyme, creeping

ground covers for banks

Cotoneaster
Crown vetch
Euonymus, wintercreeper
Honeysuckle
Lace plant, dwarf
Myrtle

ground covers for fall foliage

Euonymus, wintercreeper
Lace plant, dwarf
Oregon grape holly

ground covers for rock gardens

Artemisia
Candytuft
Houseleek
Phlox, creeping
Rat-stripper
Sedum

vines and hedges

clinging vines

Ampelopsis japonica
Bittersweet
Clematis
Dutchman's pipe
Euonymus, wintercreeper
Grape species
Hydrangea, climbing
Ivy, Boston
Ivy, English
Katsura vine
Kudzu
Rose, memorial
Rose, prairie
Silver lace
Wisteria

creeping, trailing vines

Honeysuckle, Japanese
Lantana montevidensis
Moneywort
Myrtle
Saponaria ocymoides
Virginia creeper

twining vines

Akebia
Bearberry
Decumaria barbara
Eccremocarpus scaber
Everlasting pea
Hop
Moonseed, Canada
Silk vine
Tara vine

annual vines

Balloon vine
Black-eyed Susan
Hyacinth bean
Mexican vine
Wild balsam apple

tropical vines

Bignonia
Bougainvillea
Coral vine
Glory pea
Jasmine, Spanish
Wax plant

vine berries

Akebia
Ampelopsis
Bearberry
Bittersweet
Euonymus wintercreeper
Grape
Katsura

vine flowers

Bignonia
Bougainvillea
Clematis
Coral vine
Dutchman's pipe
Honeysuckle
Hydrangea, cl.
Rose, memorial
Rose, prairie
Silver lace
Wisteria

hedges

formal, clipped
Barberry
Korean boxwood
Alpine currant
Winged euonymus
Canadian hemlock
Carolina hemlock
Clavey's honeysuckle
Midget hedge
Privet
Flowering quince
Dwarf viburnum
Dwarf arctic willow
Japanese yew

informal, unclipped
Arbor-vitae
Japanese barberry
Red leaf barberry
Boxwood
Burning bush (various)
Cotoneaster (various)
Slender deutzia
Mockorange
Ninebark
Mugo pine
Flowering quince
Rose of Sharon
Viburnum (various)
Japanese yew

arboretums and public gardens

Alabama
Mobile: Bellingrath Gardens
Arizona
Superior: Boyce Thompson Southwestern
Arboretum
California
Arcadia: Los Angeles State and County
Arboretum
Berkeley: University of California
Botanical Garden
La Canada: Descanso Gardens
Mill Valley: Muir Woods
San Francisco: Golden Gate Park
Conservatory
San Francisco: Strybing Arboretum and
Botanical Garden
San Marino: Huntington Library Gardens
San Simeon: Hearst Estate
Santa Barbara: Santa Barbara Botanic
Gardens
Colorado
Denver: Washington Park
Delaware
Wilmington: Winterthur
District of Columbia
Bishop's Garden, Washington Cathedral
Dumbarton Oaks
National Arboretum
Florida
Coconut Grove: Fairchild Tropical Garden
Immokalee: Corkscrew Swamp Sanctuary
Lake Wales: Mountain Lake Sanctuary
Georgia
Athens: Founders Memorial Garden
Illinois
Chicago: Garfield Park Conservatory
Lisle: Morton Arboretum
Louisiana
Many: Hodges Gardens
New Orleans: City Park
Maine
Northeast Harbor: Asticou Gardens
Portland: Longfellow House Gardens
Maryland
Baltimore: Sherwood Gardens
Massachusetts
Boston: Boston Public Gardens
Jamaica Plain: Arnold Arboretum, Harvard
University
Stockbridge: Berkshire Garden Center
Stockbridge: Choate Estate Gardens
Wellesley: Walter Hunnewell Arboretum
Michigan
Bloomfield Hills: Cranbrook Gardens
Missouri
St. Louis: Missouri Botanical Garden
New Hampshire
Portsmouth: Moffatt-Ladd House Gardens
New York
Bronx: New York Botanical Garden
Brooklyn: Brooklyn Botanic Garden
Elizabethtown: Colonial Garden
Great River, Long Island: Bayard Cutting
Arboretum

New York: Fort Tryon Park, The Cloisters
New York: Museum of Modern Art
Garden
Rochester: George Eastman House
Rochester: Highland and Durand-Eastman
Park Arboretum
Tuxedo: Sterling Forest Gardens
Westbury, Long Island: Old Westbury
Gardens
North Carolina
Asheville: Biltmore Estate
Durham: Sarah P. Duke Garden
Wilmington: Airlie Gardens
Wilmington: Orton Plantation Gardens
Ohio
Cincinnati: Eden Park Conservatory
Cleveland: Cleveland Museum of Art
Gardens
Mansfield: Kingwood Center
Newark: Dawes Arboretum
Oregon
Portland: Hoyt Arboretum
Pennsylvania
Chestnut Hill: Morris Arboretum
Hershey: Hershey Gardens
Kennett Square: Longwood Gardens
Philadelphia: Japanese House and Garden,
West Fairmont Park
Pittsburgh: Phipps Conservatory
South Carolina
Charleston: Magnolia Gardens
Charleston: Middleton Gardens
Texas
Fort Worth: Fort Worth Botanic Garden
Virginia
Mount Vernon: Mount Vernon, Kitchen
Garden
Williamsburg: Gardens of Colonial
Williamsburg
Washington
Seattle: University of Washington
Arboretum
Wenatchee: Ohme Gardens
Wisconsin
Hales Corner: Boerner Botanical Garden

books

A distinctive setting for your house
Alice Upham Smith / Doubleday, 1973
A professional guides nonprofessionals on
relating plants to various traditional style
homes—well illustrated.

The small garden book
R. Milton Carleton / Macmillan, 1971
Horticulturist considers all aspects of
home landscaping—for the nonprofessional.

Landscape for living
US Department of Agriculture Yearbook,
1972
Detailed articles for nonprofessionals on
various aspects of gardening and
landscaping in city or country.

Gardens are for people
Thomas D. Church / Reinhold, 1955
Professional advice and examples organized
in a thought-provoking way.

The landscape we see
Garrett Eckbo / McGraw Hill, 1969
A professional examines all aspects of the
landscape.

Landscape architecture
John Ormsbee Simonds / FW Dodge Corp.,
1961
Thorough treatment by a professional
landscape architect for other professionals—
architects, planners, etc.

Trees
US Department of Agriculture Yearbook,
1949
Contains a section on trees and homes with
descriptive articles on shade trees for each
area of the country.

Trees in a winter landscape
Alice Upham Smith / Holt, Rinehart and
Winston, 1969
Many drawings by the professional author
showing the structure of trees without
foliage.

Attracting and feeding birds
US Department of the Interior
Conservation Bulletin No. 1, 1973

Modern gardens and the landscape
Elizabeth B. Kassler / Museum of Modern
Art, 1964
Short, well illustrated view of gardens and
landscaping throughout the world—but not
small homes.

Modern gardens
Peter Shepheard / Architectural Press,
1953
Pictures and plans of gardens from all over
the world—but not small homes.

The garden: an illustrated history
Julia S. Berrall / The Viking Press, 1966

A history of garden design
Derek Clifford / Faber & Faber, 1962
Look up this book if you want a clear
British view of the art of landscaping.

glossary

annual

Herbaceous∗ plant that lives for one year only. Annuals complete their life cycles — sprouting, growing, flowering, bearing seeds, dying — within a single year. Seeds must be planted — by you or by the plant itself — to keep the plant as a member of your garden year after year.

biennial

Herbaceous∗ plant that takes two years to complete its life cycle. Biennials die after seeding at the end of two years of life.

broadleaf

Evergreen∗ plant that has a broad leaf instead of a needle leaf. Broadleaf evergreens do best where winters are relatively mild.

compost

Organic∗ material made up of decomposed plants, vegetable refuse, manure,∗ lawn clippings, and leaves (humus∗). Used as a nutrient∗ for trees, shrubs, and gardens and, when finely ground, as a top dressing for lawns. When mixed with soil, compost helps make the soil friable.∗ As a top dressing, compost helps inhibit weed growth and loss of ground moisture.

coniferous

Plants such as pines, spruces, and cedars, that bear their seeds in cones.

deciduous

Plants that drop their leaves every year.

dust mulch

A layer of finely pulverized soil created by cultivating. This layer on the ground's surface inhibits evaporation of moisture from the soil.

evergreen

Plant that retains its foliage throughout the winter or, in tropical countries, throughout the dry season.

fertilizer

Plant food, usually inorganic.∗ Most contain specified amounts of nitrogen, phosphoric acid, and potash, the three most important plant nutrients.∗ Fertilizer bags are labeled with numbers, such as 4-8-7 or other combinations of three-digit numbers, that show amount of each of these nutrients in the fertilizer. The first number is always the percent of nitrogen; the second, phosphoric acid; the third, potash.

friable

Soil that is easily dug or cultivated. It is loose and easily crumbled. Compost∗ and humus∗ mixed with soil help make and keep it friable.

herbaceous

Plant with a fleshy, nonwoody, usually green stem. Herbaceous plants usually die down to the ground in the winter. Annuals,∗ biennials,∗ and perennials∗ are herbaceous plants.

humus

Partly or completely decomposed vegetable matter. Humus mixed with the soil enriches and enables it to hold far more water than it normally could hold. (See also compost.)

inorganic

Nonliving materials. Chemical fertilizers,∗ for example, are inorganic; humus, compost,∗ and manure∗ are organic.

manure

Animal dung added to soil as a source of nutrients.∗ Adds more permanent value to soil than chemical fertilizers do, but nutrient content may not be as highly concentrated.

microclimate

Small climates existing within the limits of your property. Caused by structures and plantings that change wind patterns, create light and heat by reflection, create coolness by shade.

micronutrient

Food element essential in very small amounts to the health of both plants and animals.

mulch

Substance used to cover the ground around plants to keep moisture from evaporating and to discourage weeds. Typical mulches are compost,∗ leaves, rotted manure,∗ straw, grass cuttings.

nutrient

Nourishing substance; food.

organic

Living material. Organic plant foods, such as manure,∗ compost,∗ and humus,∗ are produced by living things.

ornamentals

Plants grown mainly for their showy flowers, fruit, or foliage. May be planted in groups or as specimens.∗

perennial

Herbaceous∗ plant that lives through more than two growing seasons. Perennials die down to the ground in winter but come up again in the spring.

pH

Symbol denoting acidity and alkalinity. A pH of 7 is neutral (neither acid nor alkaline). A pH of from over 7 to 14 is increasingly alkaline, from under 7 to 1 is increasingly acid.

pruning

Removing branches of plants to modify their shapes, encourage denser growth, encourage flowering and fruiting. See the maintenance section of this book (pages 130-131) for details about pruning.

root pruning

Removing large roots to encourage fruiting and to increase the number of fine, fibrous roots to increase ease of transplanting.

specimen

An ornamental∗ plant with special qualities — shape, color, floral display, texture — that justify its being planted alone to display those qualities.

succulents

Plants with thick, fleshy leaves or stems for storing water in dry climates.

suckers

Shoots originating from the base of a trunk, from the ground, or higher on the trunk and on branches (often called water sprouts). Should be removed, as they live at the expense of the plant on which they grow.

topsoil

The top layer of soil that is modified by cultivation and by decomposition of organic∗ matter.

woody plants

Plants with woody stems that do not die down to the ground in winter, the opposite of herbaceous∗ plants. Most of the plants in this book are woody plants.

index

common plant names

scientific plant names